AUTHOR ENDORSEMENTS

"It was with tremendous interest that I read Randy Cole's manuscript, *The Boy Under the Bed, From Familial Abuse to Redemption*. Although I have known and worked with Randy for over 20 years, I did not know all of his personal story about abuse and sexual abuse in his family. With great satisfaction, I did watch Randy's growth as a certified counselor in the sex offender program and becoming one of the best in the State of Iowa as well as being recognized throughout North America. It is an amazing story of how these experiences prepared him to be able to make a critical analysis of the familial abuse in his own family, to comprehend the complexities of treatment strategies, and apply his caring, compassionate knowledge in the treatment programs he supervised. The Good Wolf prevails!"

~Gary Hinzman, Author, Retired Director, 6th Judicial District (DCS)- Iowa

"*The Boy Under the Bed, From Familial Abuse to Redemption*-A compelling story which leads you into the world of familial abuse and the complexity of family dynamics and brings you to a result of faith, healing, and redemption. A reflection of what so many families live with privately and how one survivor and his family, through the eyes of the storyteller, found hope and healing. A story no one ever wants to live, but everyone needs to hear."

~Sheryl Hutchinson, Author

"For those who are unfamiliar with the dynamics of abuse in the family, *The Boy Under the Bed* is truly an awakening. It will make your heart cry out, and your soul thankful. For those who have been down such dark and secretive pathways, Randy's writing will offer you encouragement and hope. This marvel of a book exposes raw nerve endings and tugs at the heartstrings ... a balancing act between the cruelty of humanity and the joy of healthy, faith-filled relationships ... a genuine and inspiring prize! Randy's story is a victorious testament to the transformative power of faith and love!"

~Ron Puettmann, Author (and Brother in Christ)

"Randy's story of redemption has the ring of Booker T. Washington who said, 'Let no man pull you so low as to hate another.' Each person recovering from sexual abuse and family violence holds personal strengths that can transport them from the momentary despair of post-traumatic stress to a final destination of post-traumatic growth. Randy describes a family that wrestled with hurt and sadness, and came away with a sense of hope and deliverance."

~Geral Blanchard, LPC, Author

The BOY UNDER *the* BED

From Familial Abuse to Redemption

RANDY E. COLE

Wasteland Press

www.wastelandpress.net
Shelbyville, KY USA

The Boy Under the Bed:
From Familial Abuse to Redemption
by Randy E. Cole

First Printing – September 2016
ISBN: 978-1-68111-136-0
Library of Congress Control Number: 2016951583

Scripture directly quoted is taken from the Holy Bible, *Contemporary English Version*,
Copyright © 1995, American Bible Society, 1865 Broadway, New York, NY 10023.
Used with permission by their copyrighted directives.

Geral Blanchard quote from, *Ancient Ethics for Today's Healers,*
used with permission, copyright by the author.

Professional family portrait (Figure 2) and author page professional portrait (Figure 32)
used with permission, copyright of Lifetouch, Inc.

Printed in the U.S.A.

0   1   2   3   4   5   6   7   8   9   10   11

AUTHOR'S ELUCIDATION

During times of trauma with its related dissociation, and with the developing brain of a child, teen, and young adult, memory is rarely perfect. The brain and memory do not work that way; it looks for patterns and doesn't "memorize" details and perfect accuracy *always* fades somewhat with time. As I created this story, I tried to be cautious of these imperfections of memory over the years.

I praise God daily that He restored my life and blessed me with the family, friends, and career that He has provided. I am relieved to be set free from those dark days of my past and to be continuing on this road to redemption.

> *"I prayed to the Lord, and I praised Him. If my thoughts had been sinful, He would have refused to hear me. But God did listen and answered my prayer. Let's praise God! He listened when I prayed, and He is always kind." Psalms 66: 17-20 (CEV)*

ACKNOWLEDGEMENTS

There are too many people throughout my lifetime for me to thank individually in this book. The number of people who God has placed in my life from infancy to today to guide me, mentor me, and allow me to heal is amazing! Thank you for loving me, and for loving Jesus enough to obey his commandments; love God above all things, and love others as yourself.[1]

There are a few people who left a big footprint. They shaped my life and molded me into who I have become, personally and professionally. I am eternally grateful for their love and support. I've listed some of them here:

Craig
Lt. Colonel Mead; Captain Hogeland; Lieutenant Payne; Lieutenant Castang
Bill D.; Tom M.; Tex; Bob; Garry; Ron
Martha; George; Cindy B.; Cindy E.; Larry; Mike
Holly; Virgil; Gary; Mindy
Sam; Geral; Barb; Karl

Of course, thanking family is always important. For me, that includes immediate family, to blended step-family, to an array of extended cousins who keep in touch. We are a close bunch. Our lives have been so similar in many ways. We have survived the pain of various abuses and the joy of healing! It is a family affair. Please know that I love you all more than words can say. To my sisters especially, though, the bond that unites us as the "Brewer Street Kids" is stronger than any super glue! It has only grown stronger since our folks went to be with their Lord in Heaven. Your love and support are amazing! Thanks for the affectionate nickname of "Huey". I do love it! I don't mind that it's a comic-book misfit duck lacking in poise or social graces! His heart seems always to be in the right place; sounds like me, most of the time! Ha!

To my sons and stepsons, who wished they would have had more of my time growing up. Working in a human services profession with the demands and stressors associated with mission-focused ministry often means that our

---

[1] Gospel of Mark 12:30-31; The greatest commandments, paraphrased.

families suffer. I know you understood that I was helping others. I know you were supportive of my career. In hindsight, I wish that I had done a better job of balancing the scales of work/home/family. My wife and former wife are included here, too.

Thank God for the Sunday school bus and all of the wonderful folks at that little Baptist church. We, my siblings and I, are a miracle as a result of your collective faith and witness. The little boy hiding under his bed could never have imagined that his family would all have personal relationships with Jesus and be able to share that joy together.

I am grateful for the faith families who continue to support and encourage me:

Friday morning men's group
Saturday morning men's group
Sunday afternoon faith family; especially Joanna, who inspired me to write this story.
Thank you. God bless you for supporting me.

In closing, I hope that this book brings hope & healing in some way to anyone who reads it. I am grateful to Timothy Renfrow, owner of Wasteland Press, and his willingness to publish this story. Unless this book can bring glory and honor to God, it is meaningless. Most of the time, Corinthians, Chapter 13 is recited at a wedding. Remember, it's not just for weddings! "For now, there are faith, hope, and love. But of these three, the greatest is love."[2]

"Semper Fidelis" (Always Faithful) in Christ, my Supreme Commandant…

Randy

---

[2] I Corinthians, Chapter 13:13 (CEV)

TABLE OF CONTENTS

FORWARD

" **A** nd after the terrible flood waters had receded, God placed a rainbow in the sky as a promise to his people."[3] This story is a journey of faith, healing, and redemption through the eyes of a survivor of abuse. While you may try and imagine the pain and suffering, and empathize with the story teller, you will find it hard to believe. I know it was real, for I lived it. I am fortunate, being the youngest sister of the story, for I have very few memories of our childhood. Most of the ones I have retained are of happier times, but there are a few dark shadows which lurk on the edges. I referenced the rainbow, as it is my symbol reminder of God's love for me. I have a single tattoo, a shooting star with a rainbow trailing behind it, my badge I wear to remind myself of God's promise, the shooting star to tell me of achieving greatness with God at my side leading me where I need to go.

The more important story, the one I encourage everyone who reads this to know is; there is hope for healing, redemption and fulfillment of a happier life after abuse. "For we are all broken, in one way or another, and in need of healing." I live with this motto in my heart. I have changed and grown through my faith and by sharing my life experiences with others over the course of my lifetime. As a young adult, I was broken, and bitter, defiant of any belief life would be better. I had no confidence in myself, I was damaged and would never amount to anything. Through the course of my life I have been blessed to work in many human service related positions, nursing homes, mental health centers, senior citizen centers, to name a few. I was drawn to these places out of love for others and need to help others. The ability to be compassionate and caring, helping others to have a better life, to help them succeed and find

---

[3] Genesis 9:13; the story of the rainbow after the flood, paraphrased.

happiness, that has been my driving force. By helping others, I too learned to heal and be happy.

It has taken me a lifetime to learn who I am, who God wants me to be, and to push myself to become that person. It didn't happen overnight, it was a progression, as my brother's, of trial and error, falling back at times to rock bottom, and having to pick myself up and start over. It has been about examining my beliefs and my faith, challenging myself to learn and grow. It has been about faith and forgiveness, and mostly about the love of God and family. While at peace with who I am, I will always be a little broken, healing will be a continued process until the moment I have taken my last breath and go home to my Savior.

I welcome you to this story of "The Brewer Street Kids" and all of the other families across the generations and miles who have lived similar stories. May it help you to understand familial abuse a little better. May it help you to find positive influences and hope and faith if you have lived a similar story, or are still living in the nightmare. May it bring you courage to challenge yourself to want a better life for yourself and the strength to achieve it, and to become a positive influence for others. And if you are a professional who works with victims and families of abuse may it bring you a better understanding of the intricate weaving of these types of families so you can find the best way to help the whole family heal.

~Sheryl Hutchinson, Author and "Brewer Street Kid."

PROLOGUE

This book has been an idea swirling around in my head for a few years. The surge became a churning current when I retired from the Department of Correctional Services on New Year's Eve 2014. Having worked for over thirty-five years in the human services & correctional services realm, I've seen a lot of pain and brokenness. I've also been blessed to see a lot of healing. I've spent most of my professional career working in the area of sex offender treatment and management. That took pain & brokenness to a whole new level. Within that very specialized field, however, I have seen a hard shifting of labels from the people we supervised being called clients to offenders, specifically sex offenders. The term "sex offender" is a universally adopted descriptor for people who have engaged in harmful sexually acting out behaviors, applied with a broad brush to men or women, adults or juveniles, and those formally prosecuted or not. The term sex offender is used to describe those having real live victims as a result of their sexual crimes, as well as those viewing digital images and pornography.

I understand the universally accepted term of "sex offender." Law enforcement agencies need to manage a large group of individuals on sex offender registries. Correctional Services organizations need to monitor a large group of people on supervision. Prisons need to house large groups of inmates. From a management perspective, one universal term that everyone knows and understands is pretty useful. However, it's not very practical from treatment and monitoring standpoint. It presents a false sense of homogeneity with sex offenders. In fact, there is much diversity. Sexual abusers are very heterogeneous.

I survived the familial abuse within a family plagued with alcoholism. A family with incest abuse at its' core. My dad was not a "sex offender". That term is a legal term to describe someone prosecuted for committing a sexual crime. He was not a "sexual predator", a legal term to describe someone who has committed a sexually violent offense with a high likelihood of reoffending. The terms child molester or perpetrator may be more appropriate to describe my dad. However, these terms are typically heard in formal treatment settings within professional services. He was never in a formal treatment setting. He was never involved in professional services.

I know who a child molester is. Molesters are like the older single guy in town that some of the 12-13- year old boys knew had "dirty movies." My friend from up the street talked me into going over to a guy's house once. He told me the man was harmless. He told me I just had to see these movies. They were about sex. I had no idea what an 8mm reel-to-reel smut film was. I hadn't had sex with anyone. I was inquisitive about sex.

Out of curiosity, I agreed to go with my friend. The man reached over as the film played and grabbed my friend's crotch and made some remark about "getting hard yet." I was scared but still had enough sense to flee. I bolted! I was up out of that guy's house and away down the street! My friend caught up with me and acted shocked, too. He said that was the first time the man had touched him. That guy was a sexual abuser. He was a "dirty old man". I came home and told my folks about it. Typical of the responses back then, I got in trouble for going over there in the first place, and it was never talked about again.

I also know who a sexual predator is. I met one in 1977 as a Marine. A Marine stationed with me overseas who left the base on liberty one night and solicited a prostitute. He dragged her to a rice patty, raped her, mutilated her body, and murdered her. The confusing thing about that was that he wasn't a stranger to me. He worked alongside me in the supply warehouse. I had met his wife when she joined him during deployment. She gave birth to their baby girl overseas. He had recently put them on a plane and sent them home. He took up residency back in the barracks. He and I were both scheduled for rotation soon, back to stateside duty. He tried to talk me into going out on the town one last time with him. I refused. Instead, I tried to talk him into just drinking at the enlisted club on base. Military jurisdiction ended at the base gate. I was afraid of getting into some trouble in the village and not coming home. He acted like I was the one being paranoid. He laughed at me and punched me in the shoulder. Then, he and some buddies headed for the main gate on their "Benjo bombers"[4] (bicycles).

He didn't look like a monster. He didn't act like a predator. He was a friend. I was inadvertently caught up in the criminal investigation. He had ridden his bicycle into town that night. On the ride back to the base, blood from his clothing dripped down on the bike. The revolving sprocket splattered her blood across the frame; hardly noticeable, just little specks. I borrowed his bike to make a run to the commissary across base the next day. Investigators were trying to identify and explain another set of fingerprints on the bike other than his. All of us who worked with him in the supply warehouse, or lived with him in the barracks, were being questioned. Sexual predators are the guys who commit these types of incredibly heinous crimes.

A perspective that fits for me to identify my dad and others like him is to describe them as people who have engaged in harmful sexually acting out behavior. Some are adults; some are juveniles. Some are men; some are women. Some prosecuted; some not. Some have committed crimes; some have not. Some victimizers were also at one time a victim; some were not. All are in need of redemption. And, the universal labeling does not help them heal.

When I began my journey into sex offender treatment about a quarter of a century ago, a colleague made a remark to a professional group of people that not only surprised me but hit me like a hammer; right in the middle of my forehead. She just addressed the group with a good morning greeting and then stated, "The first thing I want to share with you before we begin is to state one simple fact to you. I'm the only person in this room that I know is not a sex offender." Talk about an ice breaker! Maybe not so much. Men bristled, women fidgeted in their chairs, and a few took a break for coffee and the restroom. The people sexually abusing our children are living around us every day with all but the inner circle who have experienced the pain knowing who they are. Most of them are not strangers. Most of them are well known to us; just not identified as sexual abusers. Her remark meant something else to me. I could remove her name and fill in the statement with my own. "Hi, I'm Randy and the only person in this room that I know is not a sex offender is me."

---

[4] A term Marines used overseas for bicycles, named after Japanese open air sewer systems.

Her remark also spoke to my own family's dirty little secret of sexual abuse. My older sister is a survivor of child molestation; incest perpetrated by our dad. I have her permission to share that detail and some of our journey in this book. No one except for those of us in the inner circle ever knew anything about it. And, as a younger sibling, I did not fully connect the dots until we were all adults. I always knew there was a different dynamic at work with the love/hate triangle that existed between her and my parents. Even different than the one that existed for me. It sounds selfish to say, but I had my survivor issues going on being a child of familial abuse. Not surprising to those of you who grew up in a dysfunctional home, there often is a myriad of abuses intertwined with alcoholism. There was plenty of violence to go around for the rest of us. In those dark days of our family's history, we were all surviving something on a day to day basis.

This book is meant to be less about dysfunction, pain, and abuse and more about healing, redemption, and restoration. It is about inspiring hope. I also want everyone reading this to know that hope exists for everyone within that inner circle, hope for the direct victims, indirect victims and the perpetrators of the abuse. Maybe we are the fairy tale family that has managed to live "happily ever after".[5] The point is that we truly have! No, our relationships are not perfect. We sometimes irritate and annoy one another. But the hate and petty jealousy are gone. The guilt and shame are gone. Whatever lingering remnants of it that surface from time to time quickly disappears into the deeper abyss of the mind. Thoughts of the love, peace, joy, and compassion that we have for each other envelopes us. For us, this kind of healing is not humanly possible. It was a gift freely given through the Holy Spirit. That gift and the healing that followed has manifested itself in numerous ways throughout our lives. This book will get into that so that you can experience the truth of Romans 8:28, too, and realize God uses all things for good according to His purpose. Even the horrible experiences of abuse that we endure that were never a part of His plan.

It is a book about faith. About me re-establishing a personal relationship with God through Jesus. That may not be everyone's journey. It is my journey. It is my belief. I laugh at friends and family when they say, "Can you not talk

---

[5] "Happily ever after" is a common phrase for the retelling of folklore, fables, and tales; especially in children's literature

about God in a conversation? Can you go for a day without mentioning God, Jesus, the Bible, the gospels? No, not really. It's woven into the relationship I have with Him now. So, for those reading this book without that relationship with God or a Higher Power, that's okay. Please don't be offended or turned off. This book is simply my story. It is my journey. When Jesus was preparing his disciples for ministry, he told them when they met a crowd outside a village that did not want to hear their message, wipe the dust from their feet and move on. In essence, this is what Jesus did when the Samaritan village refused to allow them to enter. At least two other disciples protested and wanted some type of retribution. Jesus only told them to move on. Basically, "Let's take some time to rest and go to the next town. Maybe, someone, there will want to hear about my journey and who I am."[6] He did not force himself on the people of the village. I'm not pushing my faith journey on any reader here, either. If my journey somehow resonates with you and you want to learn more; great! I would love to share more of my faith than what this book can disclose. Please contact me!

This book is for the caregivers and treatment providers; the healers who are tirelessly working to help families caught in abuse cycles. Never give up! Stay encouraged. Always have hope. Rise to the challenges of each day. You are making a positive difference! You are having an incredible impact! You are helping victims, survivors, and abusers to heal. Whether your work is in a professional or non-professional network; it matters! This book will hopefully show you how both systems can operate together, hand in hand.

This book is my story through my lenses as one of the "Brewer Street Kids" (as we have affectionately come to call ourselves). Although I have the permission of each of my siblings to write this book, it is filtered through my experiences, my emotions, and my coping responses. This story is my journey to healing. Splashes of their journeys have been included to give more understanding to the depth of the abuses, complexities of the issues, and the very distinct paths through life that we all took. Each of them would write a book that was different, although some of the events would be the same. There would be resemblances to my perceptions; other times, perspectives would be uniquely different. We are very diverse. I'm the boy under the bed. My sisters

---

[6] This passage in Luke 9:51-56 (paraphrased) is one of many that shows how Jesus wants a relationship with us

each have their story of healing and redemption. I'll leave it to them to decide if they will ever add to this book and provide their personal stories to the "Brewer Street Kids" memoirs.

The book will be like navigating a maze at times. The English, the grammar, the prose, the flipping of past, present, and future tense vernacular will keep your mind processing to decipher the information. I am specifically going back to look through the lenses of a little boy. Hopefully, most professionals reading this book will understand. Like when conducting a social history with a client, their recall does not follow a chronological script. Like traffic officers interviewing eye witnesses of an accident, there are multiple accounts of the same incident. People view events through their filters; their experiences; their senses. And, they are trying to recall events from the past. I have attempted to place things in as accurate of chronological order as I can remember, although many years later. Some dates are verifiable. Some incidents are not. The events and incidents, however, were real. There are stories handed down from people who are now dead. Respecting anonymity, except for myself and my older sister, I have only used the first names of individuals who have died.

This story is not a direct, sequential account of my life. It is a collection of memories from my life. The mind, particularly one that has endured trauma and abuse, does not store things in neat, compartmentalized reference files. Memories store in visual collages. These are collections of events and incidents throughout a lifetime. Please consider this as you read. This story is not an autobiography. It is a boy recollecting his youth and the events that shaped his journey. It is a description of the complexities of men responsible for familial abuse who became different kinds of people as grandfathers and great-grandfathers. It is a story about the marriage of two family systems plagued with generational familial abuse. God intervened to end the suffering. His plan all along was to promote healing and redemption for us; for me, the boy under the bed.

You will pick up on a few other things. I was a troubled kid. I was full of uncertainty, anger, and jealousy. These negative emotions certainly shaped my perspective at the time. Every child seems to grow up believing that their Dad can do anything. He can walk on water. He is ten feet tall and bulletproof. Those childhood perceptions become magnified in a negative way when a father is tormented and prone to episodes of abuse. The fears and insecurities become consuming. The drive to feel loved wanted, accepted, and to "measure up" overtakes. Or, some children simply feel overwhelmed and give up from a sense of hopelessness.

As I proofread this book, this realization came through like a dripping syrup! It's hard to write and harder to read. It's also complicated. It wasn't always that way growing up with my dad. Some moments and incidents were fantastic; fun, loving, caring, and accepting. Thanks to some amazing therapists like Virgil, I have been able to confront those negative emotions, reframe perceptions, and shift paradigms. These therapists (or healers as I like to say) ignored clinical labels in my counseling sessions. They did not allow any diagnosis to define me; identify me; become me. Am I completely cured? No; only healing. I am much more whole and complete than I have ever been, day by day.

Some residual consequences and trauma from abuse last a lifetime. Just like soldiers who survive wars, there are triggers and trauma bonds that affect them years later. With professional help, positive supports, and understanding, these things get better; much better! I don't know that the trauma ever ends. Trauma is probably an individual thing for survivors. When my life seems out of balance, and I am noticing much distress, I experience night terrors. Usually, there are two themes. One is of me dreaming, and in the dream, I am awakened by noise or presence in the house. Lying in bed, I quickly affirm that before going to bed I had locked doors, checked windows, and I sense that the house is still secure; no one broke in. Then a shadowy male figure enters my bedroom. I am anxious. I am afraid. I feel helpless. I cannot move. I cannot wake up. I cannot defend myself. As he approaches my bedside and leans over me, I suddenly wake up; gasping, heart racing. I never see a face. I can never fully make him out. I walk myself through the paces of realizing it was only a dream. While relieved, I sometimes have to check the doors, locks, and walk through the house to feel safe; that the intruder is gone. Oddly, though, he never came from outside the house?

The other recurrent night terror is to dream that I am driving home, and just outside of town, a massive tornado is barreling down on me in the vehicle. I stare at it. Mesmerized. By the time I realize that I have to flee, the air pressure on the door won't allow me to get out. I am frantically trying to open the door; break the window! All of my efforts fail. The huge funnel consumes me, as my vehicle spirals upward into the vortex. I suddenly wake up; gasping, heart racing. Night terrors like these were very common for the first twenty years or so of my adult life. These have subsided significantly and are rare now. I take that as a sign of healing.

A typical existing trauma bond is when someone is speaking to me, and their mannerisms, voice inflection, or tone transcends me back to that troubled boy who felt looked down upon, insecure and humiliated. When I sense that someone is condescending toward me, and acting as if they are somehow "better than me," I can become angry quickly; flash anger. It doesn't manifest as physical gestures; it is through verbal aggression and defensiveness. I think I am being judged and made to defend how I feel about whatever the issue is. As you can imagine, when this is my distorted perception and not reality, it has left people confused and trying to figure out why I reacted defensively or rudely. Fortunately, most of the time people sense that the communication is not clicking, and want to explain the misunderstanding. Or, I indicate that I misunderstood something, and would like to resolve the issue. Again, this used to happen frequently. Now, it rarely happens. Another sign of healing.

A writer has the responsibility of identifying his or her audience. That usually means identifying a primary audience as well as a secondary. The primary audience I believe God has inspired me to reach out to are people like me. Like, my siblings. Like, my family. Those individuals who have survived familial abuse, or currently caught in its' grasp. You can break the vicious cycle of abuse! You can be set free! Healing and redemption are real. They are attainable. As you will see in my story, God used unusual circumstances to bring about my healing journey.

Secondary audiences would be treatment providers, service workers, and healers. These may come from professional or non-professional backgrounds. We live and work within systems that label everything. We label everything from food groups, investment markets, hobbies, interests, and people, to name a few things. Human service agencies and criminal justice systems need to manage large groups of individuals. So, labeling people into groups is understandable. However, providing services to clients and promoting change doesn't work well in a system of classifications. This approach fosters a sense of homogeneity that does not exist. It is probably more damaging than what we understand. We fail to see people as individuals. We do not manage to see families as unique. We are not able to recognize that intricacy is the reality. We tend to seek easy answers to complex problems. Hopefully, to secondary audiences, this book will provide some understanding and further awareness. It may be something you choose to share with clients who are on a similar journey of healing as my family.

"God planned for us to do good things and to live as He has always wanted us to live. That's why He sent Christ to make us what we are." Ephesians 2:10, Contemporary English Version (CEV)

Thank you for reading about my journey of redemption.

Blessings, always,

Randy

CHAPTER ONE:

Burns Lane

September 1st, 1958 was a beautiful day across eastern Iowa! The temperature was a chilly 71 degrees; considerably nicer than the August heat that averaged 85 degrees throughout the month with high dew points and much humidity. Although it was Labor Day, my mom wasn't enjoying the holiday from the Delaware County Memorial Hospital. She often told me growing up that it was indeed a day of labor! At approximately 12:05, Dr. Mary told my mom she could finally relax. She had a beautiful baby boy. Relaxing was a temporary pleasure, though. I was a premature birth and weighed in at 3 lbs. 13 oz. I was in intensive care. I was a "blue baby" suffering from lack of oxygen. My next younger sister would share the same experience two-and-a-half years later upon her "welcome to the world" announcement. We were just lucky I guess; oxygen tents, IV tubes, monitors, incubators. I've always credited the Marines with instilling their motto of "improvise, adapt, and overcome" into me. The more I reflect, I think the Marines capitalized on a survival skill present as soon as I took my first breath of air!

In the 1950's, about 7.4% of babies were born immature and with low birth weight; less than 2500 grams (roughly 5 lbs. 8 oz.). However, about 173.1 per 1,000 of those premature babies died as compared to about 7.8 per 1,000 of all otherwise healthy infant births.[7] I was born at 1750 grams and my sister at

---

[7] MacDorman MF, Rosenberg HM. Trends in infant mortali~ by cause of death and other characteristics, 1960-88. National Center for Health Statistics. Vital Health Stat 20(20). 1993.

1500 grams, so significantly smaller than the cutoff of 2500 grams to even be considered a low birth weight. Today, neonatal care successfully helps babies 1-2 lbs. survive. For comparison, though, immaturity & low birth weight (unqualified) accounted for 18% of infant mortality in 1960, as compared to a reduction of 8% by 1988.[8] Were my parents and grandparents worried; yes! Mom said that I was not allowed to leave the hospital until I weighed at least 6 lbs. Even then, my dad said I fit in his shoebox (size 7), so go figure; still pretty small.

My older sister was two years old and toddling around at my arrival. My sister had been born in Oceanside, California (Camp Pendleton) where my dad served with the Marines. He deployed to Korea at the end of the conflict in 1953 and returned to assume duties as sergeant of the motor pool. My dad had mailed an engagement and wedding ring to my mom and told her that if she was willing to marry him to come to California. Mom was living on her own and waitressing in Cedar Rapids, Iowa. They both had their stories of surviving pain and abuse within abusive families. They set out young into the world to be out on their own. They grew up together in our small hometown. Dad had a crush on Mom in his early teens. Mom was torn between accepting or rejecting his proposal until my Grandma finally told her, "Honey, you are either going to have to go to California and marry that young man or send him his rings back so he can move on with his life." Off to California, she went. Dad was 19 years old, and Mom was 16 years old. They married on July 23rd, 1955. He had already served combat duty in Korea, and she had already been forced by my grandfather to put her baby, conceived out-of-wedlock, up for adoption. Grandpa could not face the shame brought upon the family. Life is not easy. It is not pretty. And, it's very messy. The decisions we make can plague us for a long time.

My dad and the Marine Corps fit together like hand & glove; he loved it! He worked his way up the ranks to become a non-commissioned officer with some nice perks attached. He loved adventure, thrill seeking, and proving that he could "out- best" anyone. Being enamored with his beloved Marine Corps

---

[8] MacDorman MF, Rosenberg HM. Trends in infant mortali~ by cause of death and other characteristics, 1960-88. National Center for Health Statistics. Vital Health Stat 20(20). 1993.

evaded my mom. It was an adventure at first. It was an escape from a home life that had been a living hell. It was a temporary respite.

She was a mother now. A married teenage girl who still missed home. She wanted roots for her family. She wasn't excited about continuing to live in a trailer the size of a pop-up camper. Dad reenlisted for another tour of duty. Mom packed up her things, my older sister, and boarded a train for Iowa. She left him a note saying that he could contact her folks to find them. That was a bold move for a wife in 1956. Mom certainly had spunk! I'll give her that!

Without question, Dad was a stubborn man. I don't know how long it was before he decided to join her back in Iowa. At some point, Dad decided to live without her wasn't an option. He took a trip to visit the career planner. Dad was able to rescind his reenlistment papers for separation orders. He hopped a train for Iowa. That decision would afflict my dad for many years to come. The resentment from separating him from a life he loved, would ignite a rage described as a perfect storm.

By the time I came on the scene, Dad had been doing various construction jobs across Iowa and Minnesota. He was rarely home except for some weekends. Highway and natural gas pipeline construction were booming across the Midwest and Great Plains. Mom depended on her folks a lot of the time. She wasn't as close to my dad's parents. It was a small town. They all grew up together. She knew his folks and had run around with his older brother when they were younger. Extended family on both sides knew each other. But, to say that any of them were close would be a stretch.

Grandpa was called "Colonel" around town. It was an honorary title given by members of the veteran's organizations to which he belonged. I acquired my honorary title of "Gunny" within the parole unit, although I only attained the rank of a Corporal while serving my enlistment. I was a Lead Agent, having oversight of program operations. The supervisor and other parole officers said I had a leadership style like an old gunnery sergeant. The nickname stuck and became how most colleagues addressed me in greetings, conversations, and email exchanges for the remainder of my career.

Throughout his active duty military service, the Colonel had remained within the enlisted ranks. He served in the Army in WWI and received a Purple Heart for being wounded. He received a veteran's disability pension as a result of the severity of his injuries. From what my older sister, the genealogist of the family has shared, much of the first year of his return was spent in convalescent wards of military hospitals. He was an officer of the V.F.W. and American Legion. Like many of the veterans of his era, he wore the uniforms of the veteran's organizations proudly. He never spoke of his combat experiences, and he drank heavily to medicate the pain. He served in the Rainbow Division, heralded as the most decorated combat division of the war.

I know little about his childhood. When he was six years old, his mother put him in an orphanage to be raised. She was miserable, divorced, and could not care for him. Her husband had abandoned them when he was only about two years old. She was a single mother trying to survive. He was taken back out of the orphanage to be united with his mom and a new step-father when he was twelve. What he experienced in those six years is unknown to us. However, these are formative years in a young boy's life to be dealing with abandonment issues. It is reasonable to believe there was some impact that disrupted his development, however, to what degree is uncertain. He now had a stepfather. The extent of their relationship is also unknown.

Mom seldom talked about what living with him was like as a child. She said that Grandma knew by the gait that he had walked home, what kind of night it was going to be. She knew if she needed to lock Mom and her brother in their room so he would only take his wrath out on her. One day, a concerned neighbor told the Colonel that Mom had been seen skipping school to ride around with some boys. Mom claimed it wasn't her. It was another girl who looked a lot like her. That particular day, they both wore the same red scarf bandana. When she got home, the Colonel confronted her. He refused to believe that it wasn't her. He whipped her. The beating was severe. Grandma pulled him off her. She was afraid he would kill her. Although that was the worst whipping, it was only one of many lashings with a razor strap that she survived as a result of his drunken rage. The Colonel and my mom never really mended fences. The only indication of forgiveness came when he was on his death bed dying of cancer. She managed to tell him that she forgave him. However, he wasn't willing to say that he loved her. Years later, she said she knew he did, based upon his concern for us kids. She shed a tear and said she wished he had told her. He died on July 1st, 1967. He was 72 years old. When he died, I was eight years old.

Mom's relationship with her only brother, Marvin, was also conflicted. He was older than her. She described him as the instigator of most of their childhood mischief. She was the recipient of the Colonel's wrath over it, though. She loved her brother, and yet, was clearly afraid of him. Growing up, I knew that he had served in the Navy. He got into some trouble and spent time in the brig; it was a military jail. He married a woman in our hometown who had the same first name as my mom. They were all friends growing up. Uncle Marv and Aunt Jan divorced when I was young. She re-married a wonderful man, and they went on to have a family. I shared with her step-children how God had richly blessed her with their dad and family. It is what she deserved, and all she ever wanted.

About fifteen years ago, she asked me if I ever heard from Uncle Marv. She shared with me that when they were married, he had multiple sets of identifications in his billfold; ID that was his aliases. She never knew why. She speculated that the aliases were for shady business dealings. Around the early1970's he was convicted of an armed robbery offense. Back in those days, the courts had the ability to impose a bench parole which was a suspended sentence with community supervision. He absconded. He dropped out of sight.

The last time Mom even got a call from him was 1972. He said he was driving truck somewhere in Texas or some other western territory. He was feeling depressed that night from being a fugitive. He told Mom that he thought everyone would be better off if he just drove his truck over a cliff. Dad took the phone away from her and said that sounded like a good idea. Often, strangers or police would show up to question Mom, Dad, or Grandma about his whereabouts. I remember some of these visits. The strangers were intimidating guys. So, while Dad's comment was crass, it needs to be put into proper context. The disruption in their lives from these visits was routine. Uncle Marv would call collect, late at night, and was usually drunk. After the call, my mom would be a neurotic mess; sometimes for days.

I had a different relationship with Uncle Marv. As a young boy, I was closer to him than I was to my dad's brothers. That's not saying anything bad. They had children and families. We all did things together. Uncle Marv and Aunt Jan had no kids. The "Brewer Street kids" were their children. They doted on us when we were young. A lot of the "first's" that a boy experiences with his dad, I experienced with Uncle Marv. He took me on my first real fishing trip! We went to Guttenberg, to fish on the Mississippi River. We stopped at a drive-in, close to the locks & dam, and I got the hugest ice cream cone I had ever seen! Uncle Marv was trying to get me to eat it faster before it melted. He took me to my first real baseball game in Cedar Rapids where a minor league club played ball. I couldn't have asked for a better uncle growing up. I felt safe. I felt secure. I felt loved. I felt wanted. I never knew his dark side; not until I was approaching my early teens. Even then, I had never experienced it firsthand. It was hard for me to understand how he could have robbed a taxi driver. The fugitive arrest warrant was still active when I was a newly promoted parole officer. I got the order sheet to check against my client caseload. Near the end of the printout was my uncle's name, charge, sentence, and last known whereabouts. All I could think about were the happy times I had experienced with him, as a little boy.

Uncle Marv and my dad had a tumultuous relationship, too. Sometimes they would tease each other, and it seemed like good clean fun. Other times, beneath the surface of the joking, they were seething at each other. They were about the same age. One a former Marine; the other a former Sailor. Both were about the same physical stature; not much over five feet tall with muscular builds. Uncle Marv had a slightly heavier build.

One night a drinking buddy of Dad's brought him home. It was apparent when they came through the back door that he had been in a fight. He could not walk on his own; either too drunk or hurt. The other man practically carried him up the back steps. Dad's face was pretty nasty; eye cut; swollen; abrasions on his face and hands. Dad's buddy claimed they were all drinking at a truck stop east of town, and Dad tripped over some pop crates stacked up by the men's room. Mom wasn't convinced. She talked to the owner of the truck stop. His house was further up the street from ours. His wife was one of Mom's best friends. He told Mom, "Janice, Bud was out here at the station drinking with the guys. Your brother stopped out, too. The two of them "had some words." Bud went to use the restroom, and when he didn't come back, one of the guys went to check on him. Bud was hurt. Marv was gone. One of the guys said he would take Bud home. His car is parked out at the station. I don't know any more than that." When my dad was sober and out of his stupor, he stuck to the pop crate story. Not surprising, though. He would never have admitted that Marv bested him in a fight.

We did get some closure after Mom's death. We discovered some information that suggested that Uncle Marv had been living out west for many years under one of his aliases. It appeared that he was a law-abiding, respected member of the community where he lived. He died a few years before mom's death. If this was the same person, he had become a new creation and found some peace. The night that Mom died, she was in and out of consciousness. She woke up talking about walking through beautiful gardens with Jesus. Oddly, she called out audibly in her sleep to her sister (who had died hours after she was born) and to her older brother. It was as if she was experiencing a greeting by them. A smile graced her face. When she awoke, Mom told us she had seen her sister and brother and had been with them. She was only a toddler when her younger sister died. She never saw her. She never knew her. Was it real? Had she somehow transcended a spiritual plane as God was preparing her for her death? Was it the imagining of a dying woman trying to process her final moments of life? It's a mystery to me for now. Someday, I will know.

When Mom came back from California, she had nowhere else to go other than home to her parents. She was married. Her husband was staying in California in the Marines. She had to take care of a baby girl. Not a lot of options for a teenage mom with no high school diploma and only some waitressing skills. Grandpa and Grandma owned and operated a nursing home on North Brewer Street. Grandma had her nursing degree. When Mom and her brother were young, Grandma worked at the mental health asylum in one of the neighboring towns. Grandpa worked at the asylum part-time as an orderly of some sort. When they bought the nursing home, there was a grand opening, and community members gave Grandma a beautiful Last Supper painting that hung in the lobby of the nursing home until she retired. It currently hangs on my kitchen wall.

When Dad returned to Iowa, he had a modest amount of money, no job, and was starting over. They lived in a room at the nursing home. Mom helped around the nursing home by cooking, cleaning, and doing laundry. Dad was able to find seasonal construction work that paid pretty well at the time. Between the various construction projects available throughout the Midwest, the work was steady. He was away from home for extended periods of time. It was not much different for Mom than being married to a Marine on scheduled deployments. Dad had taken to heavy drinking, playing cards, and shooting pool on the road. How much of the money made it home, versus being spent on those pleasures, remains unknown? It wasn't that he did not provide for us. It was the blue-collar culture at the time. Men worked hard, drank hard, and played hard. With seasonal construction labor and winter layoffs, the dark, dead of winter signaled our nightmares on Brewer Street that were yet to come.

With Mom expecting me, our little family was outgrowing the room at the nursing home. The Colonel found a little tarpaper shack in the north end of town called "Burns Lane" and he made a down payment with rent paid forward so we could move in. To hear my dad tell it, it wasn't much of a house; just a shed with one or two rooms and a stove. He claimed that the light shone through the cracks in the walls and windows. It was a temporary arrangement as the Colonel was figuring out a more permanent plan. It would have to do for the time being. God is good. A woman named Ollie befriended Mom. Ollie would eventually move with her family to a small acreage west of town. My older sister says that she remembers begging to go next door to play with Ollie's oldest son. My memories are limited to the farm with her younger son, and the fun we had exploring the outdoors. The time on Burns Lane was short, but the friendship with Ollie took root, and she became one of my mom's closest friends. She was a rock in the times of storm. Mom was prone to neurotic episodes and constant worry. Ollie was one of those people who could be firm, yet calm and gentle with her, all at the same time. While exciting for us as kids, trips to the farm were an opportunity for Mom to rest and unwind. She looked forward to her time with Ollie. It was one of the only safe places she felt she had to go at that point.

CHAPTER TWO:

Brewer Street or Bust

L iving on Burns Lane was never intended to be for long. Grandpa and Grandma were older and planned to retire and sell the nursing home. In preparation for that, Grandpa purchased a tiny house on the southwest side; Lincoln Street. Not quite ready to move in yet, he moved us in from Burns Lane. Like many of the streets in town, Lincoln Street was unpaved rock. Lincoln Street curved around the property in a horseshoe-like manner, and then merged back out to the main road. It was on the edge of town with nothing to the south but open fields. It was like living in the country. A big shed on the property doubled as a garage. Dad was a jack-of-all-trades, and always created ways to make money. Dad worked on cars, scrapped metal, and hunted and trapped for wild game. And now, he could raise some rabbits! He built rabbit hutches and arranged them on the southern end of the property. Rabbits were food for our consumption. He also butchered them like chickens and sold the meat. Sometimes, he sold them as pets, especially at Easter time. Having a bunny as a pet was popular at that time of year. My older sister remembers feeding rabbits and getting bitten by a bad-tempered rabbit. I was too young for memories.

Grandma experienced a heart attack in the mid-1950's, which was before coronary-artery, by-pass surgery, had even been done in the United States (May 1960).[9] If someone survived, it was as a result of bed-rest and the blocked arteries re-routing themselves. At least that is what Grandma said in

---

[9] May 2, 1960; first coronary artery bypass surgery performed in the United States

her case. Although Grandma survived, it had taken a toll on her health. She was diabetic and taking insulin daily. She was trying to eat nutritiously, and get a better balance to her life. Although Grandpa helped out as much as he could at the nursing home, his physical disabilities from the war and the mental wounds that we now call P.T.S.D. prevented him from being in any condition to manage the nursing home, either. Retirement was coming sooner than the Colonel had originally planned.

A buyer gave a good price for the nursing home, and the deal closed. The Colonel and Grandma set the short timeline for my parents on when they would be moving into the house on Lincoln Street. My folks were house hunting, again. Although I am sure that the Colonel offered to help them get started in another house, my parents wanted a home. My dad liked the little house on Lincoln Street. It was country living within the city limits. He wasn't willing to go back to renting and living in someone else's home. He also wasn't going to accept any more help from the Colonel. He wasn't afraid of hard work. That's why he always had so many various odd jobs going on. Working so much, his time of dealing with screaming little toddlers, and our tantrums, was pretty limited, too.

Grace was an older lady that owned some properties in town that she rented. Maybe she had one she'd want to sell? Dad had his eye on a little place on the "S" curve leaving town on the south side of the tracks; South Brewer Street. Like Lincoln Street, the road was rocked. The lane, bordering the south of the property, curved around a field divided with hay and corn. It was on a big corner lot with neighbors on three sides and none to the south. The property directly to the west was a small farm. The older couple that lived there had cows, pigs, chickens, and ducks.

There was an old horse stable on the property that had a big sliding barn door. There was plenty of room for Dad to build workbenches, shelves, and section off an area for some livestock of his own. He could put up his rabbit hutches and expand the operation. It was perfect! By today's standards or even the standard then, it still wasn't much. The stable was in need of much repair. The house had green slate siding. The rooms were tiny. There was standing room only in the kitchen, small dining room, smaller living room, and two bedrooms. One bedroom was slightly larger than the other. The basement was unfinished limestone rock walls. A concrete floor had been hand poured and smoothed out, though. My dad's mom, Grandma Nellie, was a green thumb that loved her gardening and flowers. Dad inherited her passion for this as well. The Brewer Street property gave him a huge lot for a big garden. There was plenty of space for flowers, shrubs, and a long narrow terrace that ran the full length of the property. He could plant various perennials like iris's, lily's, tulips, and rose bushes.

Dad paid Grace a visit with $500 cash in hand. While I don't know all of the details, she did offer to sell the place for $6,000 rather than to rent it again, which had been her original plan. He offered her the money as cash down payment and asked if she would carry the contract for the remaining $5,500. They negotiated the monthly terms, interest rate, and the contract was signed. Why she sold it on contract to Dad rather than rented, I don't know? He was charming and polite when he wanted to be. He was a handsome man and could flirt and flatter with the best of them. He was a veteran. He was a young husband, and father of two with one more on the way (next younger sister was in the oven). He and Mom both came from "good stock" and "salt of the earth" folks. Everyone knew and liked the Colonel and Grandma.

Mom's grandfather had been a county supervisor. At one time, he owned many properties including farms and houses. Great Grandpa Harry died from a massive heart attack in 1943. He was only 57 years old. The properties all got split up amongst his immediate family. By 1960, Great Grandma Jessie (Harry's widow) only owned one home on the west side of town. She rented to boarders to make ends meet. As one of my cousins put it, "I don't know what happened? Wasn't Grandpa Harry rich? I don't have any idea where it all went?" Neither do I? I do know that had he lived; he would have taken care of Mom. I'm sure of it. When Mom and her brother were still small kids, Grandma just up and left the Colonel. He moved back to the farm with Grandpa Harry and her family. Harry was a God-fearing Conservative Republican that was not going to stand for his daughter abandoning her family, regardless of the reason! He hired a private investigator who located her around Chicago, Illinois. The detective brought her back to Iowa. Harry made it plain to her that was never going to happen again! She would stay married and take care of her children! She did; for better or worse.

Harry loved his daughter and grandchildren. Family and commitment were synonymous for him. I think life would have been different for Mom had her grandfather lived. But, we don't get to control the events in life that happen, even though they impact our lives and sometimes alter our course.

Nonetheless, that little place on Brewer Street meant a home of her own for her young family, out from under the control of the Colonel. She had left the house shortly after he forced her to put her illegitimate child up for adoption. It did not matter how much she pleaded with him to let her raise the baby; he was unyielding. The father of the child also offered to marry her, but the Colonel was not having any of that, either. She was only fourteen years old!

The father of my half-brother that I have never known was always there for us. Townspeople thought that when he came home from the Army to find that Mom and Dad were married, the fight would be on! That fight never happened. He and my dad became best friends. He married and started a family, too. Our families grew up together. When I struggled to understand my dad, he was there as a kind of surrogate father. His fondness for Mom remained, and was often poured out on my next younger sister, who he affectionately nicknamed "Di-dee." When Mom passed away at the nursing home about five years ago, he paid a visit before she died. He asked for a quiet moment to let her know he was there and to tell her good-bye. I don't know what their conversation was, and frankly, I don't care. He had once loved Mom. Dad had died about ten years before. This man's wife was already gone by then, too. He was an old man wanting to heal. He had always treated Dad with respect. He had been there for my folks anytime they needed any help. I could not fathom denying his request. My sisters either felt the same way or honored the wish without protest. Life isn't easy. Sometimes we just need closure to heal and move on, even when that takes 50-60 years.

CHAPTER THREE:

The End of the Baby Boom

The house on Brewer Street was about as tiny as a place can be, and still be called a two- bedroom home. While Mom and Dad initially took the bigger bedroom and stuck us two toddlers in the tiny room, that would quickly change as two more girls joined our happy little family, completing the Brewer-street kids. The youngest girl was born in 1962 and with that, Dad bought two sets of military bunk beds from a surplus store. My three sisters and I would learn to co-habitat together in that one bigger bedroom for the next twelve years before the oldest left the nest for college in 1974. I was next to flee for the Marines in 1976.

My next younger sister was also a premature birth, born slightly over 3 lbs. My sister had to endure the same rigors of neonatal care just like me before coming home from the hospital. Dad was still working on the road and rarely home. It wouldn't be until the youngest girl was born that my mom would finally stomp her feet and give my dad an ultimatum. She had four kids ranging in ages from 6 years old to an infant! She wasn't going to do this parenting thing on her own anymore! There were simply too many kids with toddler demands to put us on a train for an adventure to see Daddy. My oldest sister had started school, and Mom enrolled me in kindergarten in the fall. While I don't recall how long it was before he quit the pipeline job and came home, I know he wasn't happy. Life on the road was full of adventure and gave him a ton of autonomy. He could rationalize that he was a responsible husband and father providing for his family. He could come home every once in a while, to see us; usually driving all through the night just to get home. He was always drunk and could not remember the trip! Then, he was back out on the road again doing God knows what! Concerning Dad's outlook on life, God wasn't even on a back burner, yet. I'm not even sure that the pilot light was on.

Like six years before, when she boarded a train and left him in California, he must have known she was serious, though. He couldn't risk losing her. He gave up working on the road and came back to our small hometown to work. It's odd that with the mechanic's school training in the military, he never took a full-time job working in an auto garage or dealership. He was able to find employment in factories. He always worked on vehicles for people on the side for extra money, though.

My older sister and I are not sure of the order, but he worked in a manufacturing plant and for the gas company. Somewhere in the mid-1960's, he took a factory job working for a hide corporation. The pay was good at the time. I remember seeing the ad in the newspaper offering starting pay at about $1.83 hr. The Hide Plant Corporation offered plenty of overtime, too, although there were periodic shutdowns and layoffs. While Mom thought things just might be looking up, they were about to get a lot worse before ever getting better. For most of the next decade, we lived in a war zone, and we were navigating a mine field. The threat wasn't from outside our home, though; he was inside. Dad drilled into us that whatever happened in that little green house, stayed inside that little house!

Figure 1: The Brewer Street Kids; circa, 1964

Figure 2: The Colonel & family. He doesn't look happy; circa, 1943;
Photo used with permission, copyright Lifetouch, Inc.

Figure 3: Train trip to Minnesota to visit Dad (1959)

Figure 4: The Colonel served in WWI with the Rainbow Division; circa, 1917; {{PD-USGov-Military-Army}}

Figure 5: My family with Great Uncle Oren; back for his father's funeral; circa, 1966

Figure 6: Older sister with both Grandpas; Colonel (left), Louie (right); circa, 1964

Figure 7: Me and my older sister with Colonel & Grandma Sylvia; circa, 1962

Figure 8: Ready to move to Brewer Street; circa, 1960

Figure 9: Mom & Dad's engagement photo; circa, 1955

Figure 10: Colonel & Grandma Sylvia;
circa,1932

Figure 11: Grandma Nellie & Grandpa Louie;
circa, 1930

Figure 12: Great Grandpa Harry; circa 1943

CHAPTER FOUR:

Pandora's Box Opened

It's taken me three episodes to be finally ready to shed some light on what happened in that little house on Brewer Street. These were important chapters to lay the foundation for understanding how complicated things like alcoholism and familial abuse are. There were generational patterns in place that were setting the stage to come.

I have spent the last twenty-three years as a professional sex offender treatment provider. Even with my personal experiences, I have been responsible for oversimplifying and making judgments. I have failed to recognize the complexity and heterogeneity of the offenders, the victims, and the families from which they came. All for the right reasons. All with good intentions. Decisions made with the purpose to serve, protect, and treat. I would like to tell you that I have no regrets about any of those decisions. I wish I could inform you that I have had a peaceful sleep every night since entering this field. I cannot say that. Some decisions still bother me. Some I have taken to God in confession, the sins of either omission or commission. I've asked for His forgiveness. I was only doing what I thought was right or best at the time.

Unfortunately, there are always unintended consequences and collateral damage with the decisions that we make. Judicial systems, criminal justice systems, and human services systems (in my opinion) are responsible for this all of the time. Again, right reasons; right motives; good intentions. However, in our quest to wrap our heads around things and understand, we tend to make the answers simple. The answers to address the problems are as complicated as the families themselves. Sometimes the systemic generational dysfunction that has become woven into the fabric of their values, attitudes, and beliefs compounds these issues further. I'll speak more about that in an epilog. For now, it is important to get back to Brewer Street.

For about a decade, mid-'60's through mid-'70's, the turbulence and chaos of the Country defined our home. The violence in our nation was front and center in our living rooms; on our television; on the radio; in our newspapers over breakfast. That was not true for the violence in our home. To the world outside those four walls, we were getting by; just another low-income blue collar family. To everyone else, we had wonderful folks that were just doing their best to provide for us and raise their children. We were not unlike many other families in that small town. The list of people in my hometown that would tell you how much my folks meant to them and the kindness showed towards them would fill a notebook! Some people will read this book and call me a liar. They will refuse to believe that Dad was capable of such unspeakable things. Some will read the book and like a puzzle fitting into place will finally be able to answer some questions that have been nagging at them for years. Some will read this book and shed tears, as they relate to the story, having grown up next door, down the street, across town, and surviving the same environment within the confines of their home. Ironically, with me not ever knowing what it was like for them, either.

I'm struggling right now even to put words on paper to describe the next decade of our lives. Because it's complicated to explain. It was everything on the spectrum from a happy, loving, fun-filled time in our lives to surviving a living hell. Where things were at on the spectrum could change day by day; moment by moment; and situation to situation. Dad could be loving and caring. He could be funny. Dad was multi-talented as well as multi-faceted. He was a happy drunk, and sometimes a violent mean drunk. At other times, he was a lunatic capable of doing things to us that were unforgettable, if not unforgivable (at least on a human level of forgiveness). The only way to describe it is to start telling it and allow you to follow my train of thought, the weaving back and forth, and circling the wagons to tie it all together.

From my perspective, Dad had not resolved the fact that he was no longer a career Marine. He had an adventuresome side that took to the lifestyle that working on the road gave him in the construction jobs. Dad seemed conflicted. I believe that he did want a family. Dad did want a home. He did want to settle down. And yet, he was at war with his flesh, much like the Apostle Paul describes in Romans, Chapter 7; "In fact, I don't understand why I act the way I do. I don't do what I know is right. I do the things I hate."[10] In many respects, it is much easier to be a long distance husband, and father than to be there on a daily basis caught up in the mix of family life. The mind knows the truth, but the flesh is weak and battling with emotions. I'm not giving him excuses. He is responsible for his behavior, and the consequences of his actions. He eventually owned that and lived for many years as a different kind of husband and father. A man who truly did all he could to make amends. He was the grandfather to our children that we wish we would have had as a father. We feel blessed and grateful for that. Hopefully, through reading this story, more families that have experienced familial abuse can one day say that, too.

Mom and Dad were young when they each struck out on their own to flee from the dysfunction enmeshed within their families. They were living on their own in their middle teens. Mom had a few older family members that helped her as she waitressed in neighboring towns. That was about it. I've talked at length about some of her family dynamics in previous chapters. The violence she had endured at the hands of the Colonel is hard to understand. Contrary to extreme violence, Dad grew up mostly lacking in parental supervision.

I haven't shared much about his story. He did not talk as much about their growing up. He was born in northeast Iowa, in April of 1936. A late spring blizzard was howling. Grandpa went out through the snowstorm to get help with the delivery. Grandma claimed that she saw angels sitting at her bedside to calm her and tell her she would be okay.

Dad talked about shooting marbles as a young boy under the one street light in the little town he grew up in as a young boy. After a few years, Grandpa and Grandma moved their family to a small town that was the county seat and lived there the rest of their lives. That is the town where I was born and raised, too.

My older sister and I have tried to piece together the puzzle of where our parents came from within their functioning, dysfunctional families. We have been met with either passive reluctance or angry refusal when trying to get any information, even when we conveyed that our wanting to know was not about hate or bitterness. We only wanted to understand what might have shaped

---

[10] Romans, Chapter 7:15 (CEV)

their lives in the way that it did. We were routinely told "let sleeping dogs lie"; "let bygones be bygones"; "it doesn't change the past." Generational family shame is a profound immobilizer. It impedes healing like closing the door on a safe and giving a spin of the dial! It will not open without the right combination. I believe that takes God. A few of us in my family have found that. Dad and Mom did. The Brewer-street kids did. Even then, some things have remained a family mystery.

Dad came from a family of four siblings; there were two brothers and a sister. He was the second youngest. His father, Louie, had a crippling disease. Shortly before his death in 1976, he agreed to be diagnosed. He had some form of muscular dystrophy. I never knew Grandpa to walk. When I was only two years old, he was already crippled. His sons built him a homemade wheelchair; a straight-back chair mounted on a two-by-four frame with wheels and casters from an appliance cart.

Although Grandpa had told us stories of driving a horse-drawn wagon that was the school bus for the rural school where they lived, by the time Dad and his siblings were teenagers, he was confined to walking with a chair that he pushed in front of himself for stability. He did have a shed out behind their home that he shuffled out to and would sharpen mower blades, tinkering with some small engine repair for folks in the neighborhood for extra money.

Given her husband's disability, Grandma worked outside the home. They needed the income to survive. Like many other women without formal education, she worked in waitressing jobs and cooked in restaurants & cafes. Eventually, she became a kitchen manager having most of the say about the food, menu, and cooking. Until she retired, she worked long and varied hours. Although she and Grandpa did the best they could, their kids had to grow up fast, with little adult supervision. Having survived the Great Depression, they had seen hard times. Alcoholism also plagued their family going back multiple generations. A few of grandma's siblings remained in the area. However, most of them had scattered like the wind across the country. I never met some of them. Others of them, I only met once at a funeral that they came home for, or a family reunion (which could lend itself to a fist fight or other ugly scene).

I was never told much about my grandpa's Dad; nothing really at all other than he farmed over by Earlville, Iowa. In later years, he owned a tavern in the small northeast Iowa town that my dad grew up in as a young boy. As for grandma's Dad, he farmed and was a carpenter. She told me that he drank heavy. He was reportedly mean, especially to her brothers. Some of them could not wait to get away from home. One brother moved to Wisconsin, another to Wyoming, and another to California.

This picture of him was hard for me to imagine. The Great-Grandpa that I knew was an elderly man in his 90's, almost blind, dark glasses, holding a cigar and a shot of whiskey in his hand. He had a wry smile and gravelly voice that gave a hint as to the instigator he probably was when he was younger. Nothing mean, nothing scary; at least not to me. I found him to be a gentle old man. My younger sisters and other young girls in the family would shy away and run to get away from him. He used his cane to hook them by a leg and pull them in for a hug. I always thought it was simply the dark glasses and smell of cigars they did not like. My older sister told me she was never afraid of him. She also only knew him to be a kind, gentle old man. They shared the same birthday. She enjoyed sitting on his lap. Maybe the younger girls were afraid because they were more shy and timid than the older girls. I don't know?

The Marine Corps drafted Dad's older brother during the Korean War. They had an uncle that lived in a town not far from the base at Oceanside, California. Dad's spirit of adventure ignited. He set out for California. He made a stop at another uncle's in Wyoming first. He was about fifteen years old. His uncle in Wyoming had a ranch. He worked as a cowboy for a while before moving on to the California coast.

Dad and his brother got into trouble involving some women, and his brother being A.W.O.L. (absent without leave). Dad's uncle shipped him back home to Iowa. The Marine Corps decided at some point to send his brother back, too. He did not like the Marines. He was glad to be discharged. Dad was totally sold on the Marines, though! All he talked about was enlisting when he turned seventeen. Although his older brother tried to discourage him, he enlisted in the Marines.

We all know sibling rivalries. This rivalry is one that would encompass their lifetime. My uncle hated the Marines. My dad loved the Marines. My uncle never liked anyone telling him what to do. That was not going to get him very far in the military. It wasn't the right fit for him. He was happy to move on from there. He wanted out. My dad didn't want to leave military life.

They loved each other, hated each other, and loved to hate each other. As the old expression goes, Dad and his brother were cut from the same cloth. Rivalry and competition consumed their lives. They were always trying to prove who was the best; who was tougher; who was smarter; who could do more; who could accomplish more. Fortunately, in the last few years before his older brother's death, they made their amends. They were finally close; maybe closer than they had ever been since they were boys. By that time, they had buried both of their parents. They had raised their children and had grandchildren toddling around. Neither one of them felt like they were invincible anymore. Neither one felt like carrying around the hurts of the past. They wanted the wounds to heal.

For lots of reasons, some real and some his perceptions, Dad seemed to have insecurities growing up in the image of his elder brother. He did not feel like he measured up. Always proving himself to others and measuring up plagued Dad. He felt less than in so many ways. That carried over into the third generation of family Marines; me. I felt the same way growing up in the shadow of my dad.

I know to some extent how violence and abuse impacted my mom's life. Not in great detail, but enough to get the picture. I don't know much about any cruelty or ill-treatment in my dad's? His Grandpa was mean towards his sons, but I never heard that this was how he dealt with any of his grandsons. When Grandpa Louie was a young man, he drank heavy. He made bootleg liquor and tied the bottles to a sash draped down the inside legs of his trousers during the era of prohibition. As one account goes, the town marshal stopped him uptown under the street light, and after visiting for a while took his cane and proceeded to break the bottles! He told Grandpa to go on home. Grandpa was pretty much known as a happy-go-lucky kind of fellow. He wasn't a fighter. Everyone liked him. He had a dry sense of humor. He had a nonchalant presentation that could address an adverse incident without the focus being on the tension or uneasiness.

There was some love/hate relationship that existed between Grandpa and his oldest son, though. That was apparent to me growing up. It resembled the same kind of love/hate relationship that I had with Dad. Nobody talked about it back then. Grandma said sometimes Grandpa could be mean when he drank. His oldest son was also a hothead. He was prone to wanting to fight over any number of things. When I was young, there was a physical altercation at a family gathering that led to them not speaking to each other for a long time. It caused division between the brothers as well. No one talked to each other. Nieces and nephews walked down the street passing an uncle without being acknowledged, even after extending a greeting. There was some deep pain that existed within those relationships, but nobody was talking about it.

As a grandson, this was hard to understand. That was not at all what I had experienced with Grandpa. He was a jokester. He was inclined to ribbing and teasing people. He sang funny little ditties that would sometimes border on inappropriate for children's ears. Grandma would scold him and tell him that was enough! He loved to play euchre. Grandpa knit scarfs, mittens, and shawls for all of us on birthdays and Christmas presents. I knew that he had been a jack-of-all-trades at one time, because he knew a lot about so many things; small engines, cars, and household repairs, even though he could no longer do the work himself.

So, go figure? Three men instrumental in my young life that had left me with a sense of security and happiness had not had the same effect on their children. At least not all of their children. I never saw any of my grandfathers' strike anyone in anger. I never recall any of them yelling, screaming, or threatening to harm anyone. I never witnessed or experienced any abuse from them. I don't doubt the accounts shared with me, albeit vague and sketchy details about most of it. These were the same men; and yet, not the same.

Dad had a different relationship with his grandchildren than he had with his children. He was the same man that had physically raised us. However, nothing about him resembled that man. I should say, none of the dark sides of his nature. The traits that we enjoyed and would only get a glimpse of is what the grandchildren grew up with as normal. That was Grandpa. He was loving. He was kind. He was fun to be around. He stuffed orange circus peanuts candy into his ears to get a laugh with the grandkids.

He was patient. He would listen. He laughed a lot. He teased and made fun of Grandma. He doted on Grandma. He loved to trout fish. He drank coffee from morning to night. He liked listening to country gospel. He gave money to charities. He sat in his recliner at night and read his Bible once in a while. He watched old black & white western movies on television that he had seen oodles of times, while Grandma crocheted in her chair. He tended his flowers. Dad worked in his wood shop. He tinkered with cars. Dad collected coins. He was a pretty wonderful grandpa. Dad was a pretty pleasant person to be around. Nothing like the man he used to be.

Dad got excited about the approaching holiday season. He got up early to dress the turkey on Thanksgiving, get a family meal started, and was like a kid consumed with anticipation as we begun to arrive with the grandkids. We would eat, visit, and sometimes play cards after the meal. At family gatherings in the warmer months, he would take someone outside to show them some new flowers or shrub he had planted that summer or fall. In the colder months, he would have plants circled in catalogs and would enjoy showing people what he planned to do with them in the spring, and discuss where they might fit into his flower beds. He visited with each of the grandkids in passing throughout the day.

Christmas was the biggest spectacle, though! He started getting decorations out early in December. He had a train that ran the border of the living room ceiling area. He had various displays out. He and a friend had made miniature lighted Christmas trees with a different holiday scene at the base of each one. He put Christmas music on as he trimmed the tree. And just like on Thanksgiving, on Christmas day he waited in anticipation for his family to come home to celebrate with food and fellowship together. He did most of the preparation. He made the goodies, treats, and fixed the meal. Mom helped him, too. It was a team operation. She was an excellent baker. But, it was mostly his thing; it was his day to serve his family. He looked forward to it every year. While many of our Thanksgivings and Christmases as kids were similar to these happy times, there was always some angst and uncertainty about the day, too. Not anymore. These holidays with them as grandparents were looked forward to by everyone. Dad especially went out of his way to make them unique, though. He wanted it to be a day that everyone enjoyed. A day that was filled with fun and laughter. Maybe, it was some penance for him. All that matters is that it brought healing for him, and for all of us, for many happy years.

CHAPTER FIVE:

The Warm Morning Stove

"Don't Come Home a Drinking with Loving On Your Mind" was a song by Loretta Lynn released 1n 1967.[11] That song was a housewife's lament to a womanizing husband. In 1967, Tammy Wynette countered with the song, "Your Good Girl's Gonna Go Bad" on her debut album.[12] I guess I would call it the housewife's warning to the womanizing husband. My last trip down country music lane is to reference Tammy Wynette's 1968 release of "Stand by Your Man".[13] This song would be the housewife's anthem to rising above the challenges of the womanizing husband.

My parents both loved country music. It was real to them. It spoke about real life. The good, the bad, and the ugliness of life, love, and relationships. Dad also had a Columbia Record Club membership at that time. We had new albums coming in the mail almost every week! The console stereo played more than the TV. Songs like those above described my mom's life a lot more precisely than Glenn Campbell's song, "Dreams of the Everyday Housewife".[14] Mom did not give up the good life for my dad. She had survived a living hell, according to her, and the few details my Grandma would ever share.

---

[11] Released by MCA Records in1967; www.allmusic.com

[12] Released by Epic/Legacy Records in 1967; www.allmusic.com

[13] Released by Epic Records in 1974; www.allmusic.com

[14] Released by Capitol Records in 1968; www.discogs.com

Although a drunken rage did result in him hitting her, as she put it, "He only hit me once. And it was with an open hand. He was drunk. He didn't mean it. And, it never happened again." From her perspective, it was not as bad as growing up with the Colonel. She had endured a lot worse. That incident will be etched in my mind forever. On a snowy, cold, Iowa night, Mom had decided (again) that she was through with him. He was drunk. He hadn't come home until late. They argued. It woke us up. She gathered her brood of kids and dressed us in our winter coats, boots, mittens, and hats and said she was taking us to Grandma's across town. He told her she wasn't going anywhere and to just calm down. She insisted that she and us kids were leaving. He refused to give her the keys to the one car we had at the time. He said she could walk to her mother's if she wanted to, but the kids stayed at home in their beds where they belonged. She marched us out the front door and across the snow covered lawn on a trek to Grandma's.

He caught up with her alongside the neighbor's driveway. He had a pair of those military white "Mickey Mouse" cold weather boots[15]. Funny what your mind will remember? He grabbed her by the elbow and spun her around. With the other hand, he swung and hit her with an open hand. The heel of his palm squares on her jaw. It took her off her feet. There was blood in the snow. She was limp. He ordered us to get back in the house. She told my older sister to get her a towel and washcloth. Her lips split. Her mouth bled. Her face swollen. She kept reassuring us that she was fine. He was still angry, but he was apologizing. He was blaming her, blaming the alcohol, and promising never to do it again. He swore he would never drink again, and begged her not to leave him. As far as I know, it was seldom talked about after that night. Night after night, Dad had been going to the tavern after work and not coming home until late. At one time, they had already separated due to his drinking and womanizing. Years later, when I was an adult, the woman told me about the short-lived affair from her perspective:

"Randy, your mother, and dad had split up for a few weeks. Your dad and I had been friends. We started going out. I remember the night that your mom came up to the tavern looking for me. She asked me to step outside. She politely and calmly told me that he was still her husband, and she was not

---

[15] U.S. government issue (USGI) extreme cold weather boots

through with him. She asked me not to interfere. She wasn't afraid. She wasn't angry with me. She only told me to leave him alone. I could not believe it. Here she was all of about 98 lbs.; she was a small woman. I had a reputation of my own for drinking and fighting. Had I wanted to fight with her over him there is no way she would have won. But, I didn't want to fight with her. I felt sorry for her. I admired her for how she handled it. I respected her for how she approached me. She asked me to step outside so she could talk to me privately. It wasn't anyone else's business as far as your mother was concerned. She had no desire to shame me publicly, embarrass me, or blame me. I told your dad it was over, and I stepped aside. He went back home to your mom."

A few years later, this same woman found herself with a toddler and a newborn; single, alone, and ostracized by much of the community. The townsfolks called this woman a shameless and immoral person. Mom would be one of the few people to reach out to her. She watched the kids for her. Loaned her money. Took her groceries. And mostly, just listened over coffee. She would later meet a wonderful man that married her and loved her children as his own. They became close friends of my folks and remained so until their death.

When Dad died, this woman gave me a hug and said, "Randy, I love your parents, especially your mom. I don't think I would have gotten through that rough time in my life without her. I could not have done for her what she was willing to do for me." She went on to say she would help Mom any way she could to get through Dad's passing. She only lived three more years herself, but she was there for Mom until the end.

I wish I could tell you that this was the only affair. The truth is, I don't know? It was the only admitted affair. I am aware that there were numerous times that his flirting, joking, and sexual innuendos toward other women upset Mom. Most of the time she tried to play it off as harmless fun and too much to drink. It was just him being the way that he was. But not always. Sometimes it apparently bothered Mom, and she had her doubts. A couple of times at the work gatherings on farms, I happened to turn a corner of a building or come out to a car at the wrong time. I caught Dad in questionable situations with women more than once. She would be startled. He would get angry. Although dressed, I had interrupted something. How far it went, I don't know? He had that reputation of being a womanizer.

On the good nights, Dad was home at night and after dinner, he would put record albums on the stereo; six albums at a time on the spindle. He would grab Mom around the waist, dance a two-step across the living room, with him singing to the music. Mom would laugh. They would hug & kiss. She loved to dance. Those were the good nights.

On the not-so-good nights, Mom would have dinner on the table, and after not hearing from him, she would feed us and get us busy doing something. Then, she started calling the local bars. Sometimes Mom reached him; sometimes not. Sometimes she waited for him to come home, and put us to bed. Other nights, Mom was either more worried about him or mad. She got our coats and marched us uptown to find the car. Mom put us in the car, found him, and tried to convince him to leave. Sometimes she convinced him. Sometimes she came back out of the tavern alone and drove us home; leaving him to get a ride from a drinking buddy or whoever would bring him. We weren't the only kids sitting in cars or playing alongside the curb. There was a group of us that routinely met under those circumstances. We played games, tag, and ran up and down the street laughing with each other. That was our normal. That was life. We didn't know anything different at the time.

We walked on eggshells back then. We never knew what to expect; drunk or sober. There were times that we played games like "Monopoly"[16], "Rummy Royal"[17], "Dealer's Choice"[18], or a homemade version of the marble & dice game "Sorry"[19]. We went to someone's house to play cards with another family that was also visiting. Sometimes, we went to a friend's farm to visit, which usually involved us kids playing outside while parents played cards. On weekends, we took road trips to visit relatives out of town. We spent one summer making day trips on weekends. We piled into the back of a huge station wagon with our cousins. Those were some great family times. That's what makes it so hard to describe growing up with abuse in a way that makes sense.

---

[16] Parker Brothers board game now Hasbro; originated in 1935

[17] Vintage board game made by Whiteman; circa early 1960's

[18] Vintage used car sales board game by Parker Brothers; circa early 1970's

[19] Parker Brothers marble board game adopted in 1934; now Hasbro

We spent days getting up early and were on the road for northeast Iowa, with stops planned at Spook Cave, Pikes Peak, the Bily Clock Museum, and the Little Brown Church. A cooler packed with sack lunches and sodas. Everyone had such a good time; kids and adults alike! We got back, pulled out an Iowa road map, and started planning the next day trip! These were some of the happiest times as young kids. Sometimes people think that when you grow up with familial abuse, it's never happy. That's not true. I venture to guess there were happier times more than the times that were not. When it was bad, though, it was terrible. As much as I've tried, forgetting those awful times has been impossible.

On those bad nights, Dad spent most of his time out in the horse-barn-turned-machine-shed scrapping out metals and working on projects. He didn't want to be bothered. I'd call these "dry drunks."[20] He was moody, irritable, and totally unpredictable. It was the same way when he was drunk. He could be fun, jovial, and acting silly. He could also become angry without warning. The slightest things could seemingly set him off.

On one of those particular nights, I slipped on his cowboy boots and strutted out to the shed to see what he was doing. I was trying to get attention. I did, but it was the wrong kind. He slammed down what he was doing on the workbench. I started to run for the house. He called it a "paddling." I call it a beating. No kid should have to go through that. Better me than my sisters, though.

While in therapy in my adult years, it was explained that often a fear of the unknown, and the impending sense of looming violence, is more immobilizing than the actual violent event itself. The terror of not knowing when the attack is coming distresses the person more than just getting it over with, so life can go back to some feeling of relief and normalcy. I provoked his wrath often as a kid. Much more than my sisters or Mom. I often got blamed for being the instigator of the sibling quarrels and squabbles, and he would single me out for most of the punishment. It makes sense to me now. This behavior was another way to try and protect my mom and sisters. As a kid, there are not many options. When he would blow up at me, he either calmed down, and left everyone alone for the night, or he used it as an excuse to storm off for the town

---

[20] A term describing alcoholics during times of abstaining from drinking

to get drunk. Either way was a win. He usually consumed so much alcohol that when he got home, he was in a stupor. It wasn't uncommon for someone to drive him home or that he needed help to navigate the back stairs. He wasn't usually in a fighting mood. With the condition he was in if he swatted at my older sister or me, he was pretty easy to push over. He was usually nearly passed out coming in the door. One night, he slept in his car in the city dump. He was too drunk to drive and navigate the "S" curves on the road. He put the car off in the ditch at the landfill entrance. The sheriff came by and left him sleeping there. He did have to pay a fine for illegal parking.

Common to an alcoholic home, after the kids went to bed, there was arguing, yelling, and fighting. It was not usually on the nights of being drunk; he was often passed out. It was the next couple of nights after swearing off the alcohol and trying to get back to a pretend normal existence. In the winter months, I often woke up to hear the commotion. After my folks went to bed, I would drag my pillow and blanket out to the living room where I would lay down in front of the blower on the Warm Morning gas stove. The stove had a window that displayed the flames. It reminded me of a fireplace with the heat coming out of the blower. The flames gave off just enough light that the room was not quite dark.

I felt safer sleeping in front of that stove than anywhere else in that house. I did not like the dark. I still don't like the dark. I prefer night lights being on. I did not feel safe in my bed, even though I shared the bedroom with my three sisters. Throughout my adulthood, I have often taken pillow and blanket and pulled up a spot on the floor in front of a heat register with a nightlight glowing in the background. Even today, my safest place to fall asleep is in our downstairs den in front of the fireplace with a pillow and blanket; the glow of a flame and the warmth of the heat enveloping me. I'm sure this is a residual trauma bond.

Another thing odd about those nights in front of that stove was how Dad got up in the middle of the night and crept into our kid's bedroom. I would be blocking the floor between the blower on the stove and the bedroom doorway. I awoke with him tripping over me; he was cussing, swearing, jerking me up, and telling me to get back into bed. Sometimes the racket would wake up Mom, and she would come out into the living room to see what in the world was going on.

As often as I could, I persuaded one or more of my sisters to drag pillow and blanket out to the stove with me, which made him even angrier. I would also routinely sleepwalk back then. Dealing with his wrath didn't stop me from sleeping in front of the stove. I still felt safer in front of the stove than in my bed or in our bedroom. And, I could somehow sense that my older sister felt safer then, too. At the time, I did not know why. I was confused. I was reacting to something. But what? Twenty some odd years later, I would get a phone call, and then, it all became clear. The pieces of the puzzle would come flooding in for me.

CHAPTER SIX:

Fortress under the Bed

As a young boy, the safest place for me during the daytime in that house was under my bunk bed. I would pull boxes of toys and books around the perimeter of the bed to close off the opening. I had whatever toys I wanted with me. Or, a book, coloring book, and stack of comic books with a flashlight when needed. I liked to read. I could put myself into the book, or even the comic book, and pretend that I was there. Anywhere but where I was. I loved the world of my own under my bed. Where no one would find me; no one could touch me; no one could hurt me. Often, when my mom would call me and be searching throughout the house and the yard, I liked not being found. That is, at least until she finally came and pulled boxes out of the way and would ask me why I didn't answer her. Although she thought it was odd that I was under there so much of the time, I wasn't hurting anything, and it was one less kid to keep track of for her. It made it pretty easy to find me.

Looking back, sometimes it was a dissociative thing. The daytime may spark some argument about the drunken night before. With not knowing the mood Dad or Mom would be in, it was safer to crawl under the bed, build my fortress, and get engrossed in a comic book or scholastic reader. I could escape into the story and become so immersed in the plot that I was tuning everything else out. What only seemed like minutes would elapse into hours as I traveled the world in my mind; from a pirate to outlaw, to the soldier, to an explorer. My favorite scholastic reader was "Mystery in the Pirate Oak" by Helen Fuller

Orton. I could put myself into the adventure with Chad and his sister Ellie.[21] There is probably a connection to this story and me starting a stamp collection.

When we went to Sunday School each week, we also were given a lesson pamphlet that would have a Bible reading, personal story from someone, or Bible story from somewhere around the world. I would often take these with me under the bed. There were pictures to color. I liked reading the stories. I would put myself into the Bible story and imagine being swallowed by an enormous whale, or climbing a sycamore tree to see Jesus, or eating fish and bread on a hillside with Jesus and the disciples. I would try to imagine Jesus touching someone and healing them instantly! I would read the stories from children in other countries like China and Africa, and how the missionaries told them about Jesus. I got the sense that Jesus did love all of the little children around the world, even me and my sisters.

Another fun adventure under the bed was to look through my stamp albums and sort through old envelopes with circulated stamps attached. As kids, we were often called "dump rats." The city dump was a paradise of lots of neat things other people threw away! My dad was a dump rat, too, and so whenever we were taking out the trash, he would pull the car over and spend some time rummaging through the debris to see what he could find. We learned to do the same thing. I got interested in collecting stamps, probably for the same reasons as reading. Stamps tell stories. Stamps provide history lessons, geography lessons, and commemoratives of everything imaginable! I found good albums, partial albums, and letters galore with different ones attached. I sat on the bedroom floor, fastening the hinges and putting it on the album. Then, I could lay underneath the bed and look through the album, putting myself into the story of the commemorative. Stamps honored industries, authors, wildlife, arts, music, theater, states, wars; stamps honored everything. It was a place to get lost for a while and not be in the little cracker box house, with the yelling, fighting, tensions, or the silence of a truce called. When I left for the Marines, I gave my stamp albums to my younger cousins. They were interested in collecting, and I rationalized that I might get killed overseas and not come home. I liked the memories of stamp collecting so much that I started another stamp album when I got back home. I still have it. I

---

[21] Main characters in the book. "Mystery in the Pirate Oak," by Helen Fuller Orton, copyright 1949; 5th edition 1967

bought another paperback of "Mystery in the Pirate Oak". Reading it periodically as an adult has helped me to laugh, smile, and relax.

Toys under the bed were small toys; matchbox size cars, farm animals, Army men, cowboys, and cap guns. Four kids were sharing the bedroom, so none of us had much room for many toys. I had to store mine in cardboard boxes that could fit under my bed. A lot of times, retreat under the bed was on rainy days or during snowy winter weather. When the weather was nice, like in the summer, I often walked out into the neighboring field with some toys or a book. An old abandoned stable was in the field, and the tall prairie grass had grown up around it. The stable still had old horse tack hanging from the inside walls; bridles, reins, and harnesses.

On a warm sunny day, laying down in a bed of prairie grass looking up into the sky with white billowing clouds and opening a book to read, was an adventurous escape that was incredible! I could shut out the rest of the world for a little while. Sometimes, the warmth of the sun made me sleepy, and I dropped the book to my chest and dozed off into a peaceful slumber. Like under the bed, I felt safe hidden in the tall grass, with the bright, warm sun rays cascading down. It is still easy for me to take a walk in the woods, sit against a tree, and go to sleep with the hot sun beating down upon me; keeping me warm; keeping me safe.

CHAPTER SEVEN:

Driving Lessons

By the time my older sister was fourteen years old and got her learner's permit, I was not quite twelve years old. When not in school or doing my chores, I was riding my banana seat bicycle made from salvaged bike parts from the city dump. Or, I was playing sandlot baseball, neighborhood football, fishing at the river with friends, or hanging out at the city park where the public swimming pool and tennis courts were. I had far more freedom than my older sister; a fact that would remain until she left home and went to college. There were also enough years between our younger siblings and us that they claim not to remember much of the abuse and violence.

Through the eyes of a child, I could not fully understand the familial abuse. I was often scared, confused, and anxious. I did not consciously pick up on the fact that my dad was sexually abusing my older sister. Through adult lenses, things have become clearer. Things made no sense to me as a child. I couldn't understand the dynamics at work. Even kids have survival skills, though. Whether for self-preservation or out of avoiding embarrassment, there were things we did that were unwritten rules; these were unspoken protocols.

We never had school friends and playmates over to the house. I did not invite friends down to my house or have friends stay overnight. If some of the guys from the neighborhood followed me home to get my ball glove or football, I told them to wait outside for me. If they suggested staying overnight, I said that we did not have the room, which wasn't a lie. I did not want someone experiencing my dad in a drunken or angry state. I also did not want to explain my mom's condition, which was often being medicated with some sedatives and feeling "out of it" for lack of better terms. As an adult looking back, I understand her anxiety disorder and neurosis. As a child, we only knew that Mom wasn't well. She was often sick and in bed. It was safer to ask to stay overnight at a buddy's house. I usually got to go. After the Colonel died and Grandma lived alone, I would often volunteer to stay with her. She doted on me. She also gave me responsibilities like mowing the lawn, taking my wagon and a grocery list to the corner store, or delivering something to a neighbor. I know she missed my uncle. She usually would slip and call me by his name. Eventually, I stopped reminding her that I was her grandson and not her son. Our relationship was more like a mom and son.

One of the most vivid memories of my grandpa, the Colonel, is sitting on his lap in his blue overstuffed chair in the front room. He smoked a pipe, and the smell of the pipe tobacco was on his clothes. It was a sweet smell. He had huge hands and long fingers. When he wrapped his arm around me and laid his hand on my leg, I felt safe. On this particular afternoon, Grandpa said something odd to me. He said, "Rand,' in a little while I am not going to be here anymore. I'm going to be up there (pointing to what I understood to be the north end of town, which is where the cemetery is). You are going to have to take care of your sisters. You are going to have to protect them." I had no clue what that was all about as a seven or eight-year-old boy, but I seem to recall nodding. That was that. Nothing more was ever said about it. I don't remember him saying anything about taking care of my mom or grandma; just my sisters. He was diagnosed with cancer a short time later. Although they operated, the disease was already too far advanced. According to what my folks told us, the doctors opened him up and said there was nothing they could do. Grandpa's cancer had metastasized to multiple vital organs. He never came home from the hospital. Mom and Grandma knew he was sick. He was a naturally thin, lanky man, but he had lost quite a bit of weight. They finally convinced him to be seen at the Veteran's Hospital, but it was already too late.

I still think that it is eerie that he asked me to take care of my sisters and told me to protect them. Protect them from what? What did he know? What did he sense? Did it mean something specific, or was it a general directive because he was aware that he was sick, and he just needed to process his mortality? I don't know?

In every family, there are roles to be played. In dysfunctional families; abusive families; there is a lot of shaming and blaming. Love/hate dynamics are typical. I loved my dad. I hated how he treated me at times. I was the recipient of most of his physical abuse. One of my younger sisters (as an adult) recently commented at a sibling retreat about how she could not understand how I could get beat and not even cry. She recalled a vivid incident from our past. Dad had me pinned up against the door paddling me for something. My sister cried just reliving it. She said, "Those weren't spankings." The force used was extreme. Sadly, by the time she was old enough to remember, I had either grown numb to the pain or refused to give him the satisfaction of seeing me cry.

As kids, we did not know what abuse versus a spanking was? Getting slapped, backhanded, paddled, or whipped was just all part of discipline for having done something wrong. We did not know that mouth or nose bleeding, cuts, or bruising were not supposed to be part of it. We could also look to other kids in our peer circles and see where they got disciplined far worse than us. The injuries they wore were more severe than ours. They were the children abused. Not us.

My best friend and I have talked about this. His dad and my dad were close friends. We spent a good amount of time out at their farm. Much of it was fun! His father owned a salvage yard, and we would play hide & seek amongst the cars. They had horses, and we would ride them often. In the winter, we would sled on the hood of a car down the hillsides. They had timbered woods, and we would squirrel hunt. The river was close, and we would walk down and fish. Both men were stern when it came to discipline. Oddly enough, his dad never physically punished me, and my dad never physically punished him. At worst, we got grabbed by our upper arm, jerked to a chair, and sat down for a scolding. His dad could be a stern, harsh man when it came to disciplining him and his brothers, though. There was no sparing of the rod.[22] Sadly, corporal punishment was taken to an extreme at times as a result of anger, pride, or frustration. Just the same, his dad had an infectious smile and a guttural belly laugh that just exploded when he was in a good mood. There were many good memories for me on their farm.

When my older sister was in therapy as an adult, the therapist asked her what her most traumatic memory was of her childhood. Without hesitation, she recalled an incident when my dad whipped me with a bullwhip for not

---

[22] Proverbs 13:24 references sparing the rod when disciplining children

getting up from the table fast enough to start doing the dishes. It was that kind of unpredictable, instantaneous rage. He told me it was my turn to clear the table, wash & dry the dishes. I answered, "Yes, sir." But, I did not get up and get moving right away. He kept the bullwhip in a chest in his bedroom closet. He yelled, "I told you to get up and do those dishes!" I heard the whip crack! I was up and moving; not fast enough, though. The whip made contact several times. My mom ran to the kitchen and intervened. She screamed, "Bud!" She put herself in the way and helped me up from the kitchen floor. I'm glad she interfered. It reduced the number of lashes I got across my back and legs.

Sadly, it probably reminded her of her painful experiences with the Colonel and the razor strap when she was a girl. Dad simply played it off as disciplining me for being lazy, and that the next time I better get up and get started on the dishes when told. Mom affirmed that in the future, I had better do as my father said. My older sister still cries reliving the incident. My sister felt helpless watching the whipping unfold. She wished she could have stopped it. The reality is that there was nothing she could have done. Just like how I could not stop her horrible ordeals.

My worst memories as a child were when Dad would take my older sister out for "driving lessons". She had gotten her learner's permit. She turned fourteen in May 1970. The car was a 1965 Chevy, 4-door, Impala; the car was white with blue cloth interior. It was usually a weekend or early evening, and he would tell her to get her permit and get in the car; they were going for a driving lesson. Sometimes she wouldn't want to go, and he would insist. He would angrily state that she had to know how to drive to take driver's education classes. He made it clear that the driving lessons were not optional. What still haunts me today are the times that she would plead with me to go along.

"C'mon, Rand.' Get in the car. Come with us. Please!" She was crying, begging, pleading. That made my dad angrier than he already was at her for stalling. He would order me to stay out of the car. Or, to get the hell out of the car had I already jumped in. She would continue to beg and plead for me to go. Mom would hear the commotion and come to the door to ask what in the world was going on? My sister would say she wanted me to go in the car with them. I would say I was okay with going. Dad would say that it wasn't safe. He was not going to have anyone else in the car while she drove on a learner's permit. Dad had to focus on teaching her to drive; the road; all of the other driving issues. He didn't have time to pay attention to another kid in the backseat or someone else to distract her. Although my mom would sometimes state that she didn't know why it would be a problem for me to ride along, she knew "the look" as well as I did. The discussion was over, or there would be hell to pay. Mom would concede, and tell me that Dad was probably right. She would usually end with, "If you don't have anything to do, there are plenty of things that I can find for you to stay busy."

In those moments of watching my older sister pull out of the lane for her driving lesson, I felt utterly helpless. I was powerless to do anything. I felt like I had somehow failed her. But, as an 11 year- old boy, I did not know how or why? When I finally understood what was going on, I felt devastated. Guilt and shame riddled me. I was angry at myself! I put those same lenses of a middle 30's man on that 11 year- old boy. I did the same thing concerning the incident in the snow with my mom. I put the lenses of an adult man on that little boy who struck out at his father's legs. I blamed myself for not stopping him from assaulting her.

Fortunately, an excellent therapist named Virgil worked with some props to recreate those situations and gently teach me to see those conditions through the lenses of the boy that I was, and not the grown man sitting before him. He allowed me to understand that there wasn't anything that I could have done differently in either of those situations. I wasn't at fault. I hadn't done anything wrong. He helped me realize that sleeping in front of the stove and blocking the bedroom doorway was probably a coping response. It was one of the only things that I could think of as a child to protect my sister. He called it a survival skill just like building my make believe fortress under my bunk bed.

My sister told me that as they would pull away in the car, he would tell her that priests did these things with girls in the church. He said that Amish Dad's did these things with their daughter's to prepare them for being older. It was to protect them from someone that would hurt them. She knew it wasn't true. Our pastor at church had never done anything like that to her. We often visited a neighboring Amish settlement to buy baked goods and groceries. We had an aunt & uncle that lived next to the colony and often had Amish neighbors on their farm. None of the Amish men had ever tried to do anything like that to her. None of the other adult men in the family had tried to do anything like that to her.

She knew it wasn't right, but she could not stop it. She thought if she would gain weight and get fat, maybe then he would just leave her alone. It seems more than coincidental that she and I have both battled morbid obesity throughout adolescence and adulthood. I was fortunate to have an interest and desire to play sports. It was a way for me to try and fit in with peers and garner acceptance, as well as a natural way of managing the weight. Even as a Marine, though, I was placed in distinct fitness platoons. The weight gain was a constant struggle then, too. My sister did not have those outlets. And, as a young girl, she believed that being obese was somehow going to help keep her safe. That is a pretty common experience for incest survivors.

When she became a teenager, her body betrayed her and physically she felt pleasurable sensations when he abused her. She was overwhelmed with guilt and shame. She told me she felt like a conspirator to the sexual assault. Not surprising, she entertained blackmailing him, too. She had not been allowed to do much of anything except help teachers with their projects at school. She was never allowed to stay overnight at a girlfriend's; never allowed to date, or go to school dances. When she finally threatened to tell someone about the sexual abuse, she was able to negotiate overnights at her girlfriend's home. She was also able to get permission to go to school dances with her friends. Usually, the caveat was that Dad told her that I had to go along to make sure she was going to be okay. Perfect for me! Her girlfriends liked me and didn't mind me going. Sis' just played it off to her friends as Dad being over-protective. Nobody seemed to question it. I didn't think to challenge it. He was always talking about the things that could happen to girls if they weren't careful. Besides, the bonus for me was that I had a crush on one of her girlfriends.

My older sister welcomed me tagging along! She was finally getting some freedoms. She wasn't a prisoner in her home. She kept the secret and didn't tell, not even to me. So, everyone was a winner; especially Dad. Obviously, as adults we all know that isn't true. Nobody won anything. As a kid surviving incest abuse, though, it sure seemed that way to her at the time. She had no control over what he did to her. The one thing she could try to have some control over was getting something out of it for herself. It sounds similar to the stories I've read from prisoners of war. Survival meant trying to negotiate with captors. We know about the trauma prisoners of war experience for a lifetime. Why would we think it would be different for survivors of incest and familial abuse?

The blackmail had an even uglier side, though. On at least one occasion, Dad offered to pay Rhonda money for the exploitation. She told me it made her feel like a prostitute. She always knew what he was doing to her wasn't right. But now, with the blackmail playing out, it had escalated to a cold and callous level of a business transaction; devoid of any feelings or semblance of any love or caring. She blamed herself for this. It was her fault.

As an adult, she knows the truth. It was not her fault. It was all a part of the manipulation and plan to control her. It's easy to see how she distorted her thinking around this issue, looking through a young girl's lenses, though. She just wanted the incest abuse to stop. Finally, when she graduated from high school and left for college, it did end. Well, kind-of-sort-a-stopped. The actual incest abuse stopped. For a while longer, though, he occasionally suggested to her that maybe they could "do something" some time, or just "go somewhere" for a ride together. She would become visibly shaken; upset, and tell him to stop. He acted like he did not mean it. He said he was only joking. He said he was just teasing her. He would apologize and tell her that he did not mean to upset her. And, life went on.

CHAPTER EIGHT:

Revival

With so much talk about all of the brokenness and pain we were experiencing, it is probably time to share some examples of the hope! Although we did not fully understand it at the time, God had never abandoned us. He had never forsaken us; not any of us. The people He put into our lives to promote healing is remarkable. And, it started when we were very young. Our grandmothers both had a strong faith in God. Prayers at meal time, prayers at bedtime and daily time for devotion were the norms when staying overnight with either Grandma. Both Grandpa's had bibles set out on bedroom nightstands, too. Sunday mornings brought television evangelists into their homes. There seemed to be a strong connection to their faith.

However, if my folks had established a previous relationship of their own with God, they had apparently drifted away. We did not pray as a family. We did not read the Bible. We did not go to church as a family. At least in the late 1960's, something about their mother's faith must have resonated with them. They made going to Sunday School mandatory for us kids just like going to real school. For the most part, no excuses and no absences. It may have been the convenience of the Baptist Church having a Sunday school bus ministry that picked kids up all over town and dropped them back off. With four kids and all in grade school, it was probably the only time that my folks got to sleep in or have any quiet time of their own. I think they looked forward to Sunday mornings more than we did! For us, it was an adventure. For them, it was an escape offering about 3-4 hours of rest and whatever.

My sisters and I tend to think it was the Holy Spirit that nudged our parents to put us on that Sunday school bus. We lived in a small town. As small towns go, it is pretty hard to hide all of your dysfunction and problems from other people. Rumors circulate; things spill over into public settings. Some people knew my dad drank a lot and spent quite a bit of time in the taverns. People knew about my mom giving a baby up for adoption when she was young, and the drinking problem the Colonel had. While I am confident they did not know about the sexual abuse or familial abuse, at least a handful of people at that Baptist Church knew that we were a family with problems. God put it on their hearts to mentor us, take us in under their protective wings, and to love on us; even our parents. I don't know how else to describe it. Individual men reached out to me, while their wives and other women reached out to my sisters. We all had different adults in the church that we became close to and who we learned to trust. We all felt loved, cared for, and accepted. Each of us had different families that we felt adopted into and taken in by them.

These adult church friends also stopped in to visit with our parents. Never to judge or call them out on their behavior, though. It was always just to visit, invite them to church, and to ask permission to include us kids in fellowship beyond Sunday school. Things like Bible camp, summer bible school, pool parties, and church picnics. My folks were invited and welcomed to go. Even if our parents weren't willing to attend, this group of adults still picked us up, took us to these events, and then got us back home safely. These church people were the closest thing to unconditional love that we had ever experienced. We felt safe with these church families, and we looked forward to it all! We were loved, praised, and encouraged. We were told that we had a Father in Heaven that loved us more than we could imagine. We learned about Jesus, and how He wanted to have a personal relationship with us. We were baptized and went through confirmation classes. We made friends with their kids. We had a church home that was not like our real home. It was like what we wanted our home to be, and we were starting to pray for that to happen.

For quite a few years, our folks only came to the traditional holiday children's programs; Christmas and Easter. We were always excited to get them there. Although my dad was not ready to conquer his demons yet, he was sometimes sober for months before a relapse. And each attempt at sobriety seemed to last longer. He was home more. He was engaged with the family more. He seemed happier much of the time. Things were slowly starting to change.

In the early 1970's, an evangelist came to church to put on a weeklong revival. Every night of the week he was preaching and singing. As a promotion for the youth group, the church sponsored a Bible verse memorization contest. They were giving away an autographed record album of his called "The Spurr of the Moment."[23] I decided that I was going to memorize the most bible verses and win that gospel album. I recited Bible verses to anyone willing to listen. I was so excited when I learned that I had memorized the most verses! The album was presented to me on a night of the revival. I was able to guilt my mom and Dad into coming to see me get the award. Long story short, my mom answered an altar call and gave her life to Christ. Although things did not immediately change overnight, her life had begun to change. And, one of the Bible verses I memorized became etched in my brain, "God will bless you if you don't give up when your faith is being tested. He will reward you with a glorious life, just as He rewards everyone who loves Him."[24] Battling temptations have been a huge obstacle to my discipleship. I think God knew how important this verse would be to me for the rest of my life.

Mom also had a girlfriend that was a housewife that lived up the street. Mom's friend was a few years younger than my mom, had two little kids, and a husband that also had a drinking problem and the sundry of related issues that come with it. Mom took her in, or vice versa and they had a daily coffee connection wearing a path between the houses. In the next few years, she also connected with another woman in town that was a friend from their former drinking days. Her husband was sober now thanks to A.A., and she was involved in a group called Al-Anon; support for the non-alcoholic spouse. She and Mom also had coffee from time to time. Although my dad did not join A.A. yet, he was staying sober most of the time. When he did relapse, it was short lived, and the next stretch of sobriety would be longer.

At some point, my folks reconnected with another couple they had known from the tavern scene. Only now, he and his wife were sober and also born again believers. They were members of a church in a neighboring town. This couple had previously been in a country & western band in their honky-tonk days. Now, they traveled around the Midwest performing in a country

---

[23] Theron Spurr was the evangelist, musician, and performer

[24] James, Chapter 1:12 (CEV)

gospel band. Through this reconnection, my dad began considering the process of committing his life back to Christ, although in a private and personal way rather than the altar call involvement Mom had experienced. This period was about the time I was graduating from high school and leaving for my enlistment in the Marine Corps. God had a plan. He knew that my dad was going to need to be sober and have stability before I came back home out of the military. My dad was still in the infancy stages of his new creation transformation, but the spark had ignited. Although it was not burning brightly, the spark did not extinguish. However, most of the change happened while I was away. I returned home from the military to quite a different Dad. That took a while to accept and believe.

CHAPTER NINE:

The Prodigal Years

I had issues with Dad; feeling less than, never loved, accepted, or measuring up to who I thought he expected me to be. Some of this was false perceptions in my mind, and some of it was the truth. He confirmed that in later conversations as we both were sober and worked to heal our relationship. I wasn't the kind of son he wanted or envisioned. As a younger boy, I was shy; timid; reclusive. I was not strong or muscular. I did not have natural skills and abilities surrounding coordination, dexterity, and motor skills. I was left-hand dominant. Teaching me how to do anything was a frustrating struggle for him. I held tools wrong. I approached things in a backward kind of fashion. Growing up left handed in a right handed world was awkward.

In third grade, I had a stern disciplinarian teacher that tried to break me of being left handed. She forced me to seek to use my right hand to do everything; cut, draw, write. I could not do it. I failed. She intended to flunk me and keep me in third grade. Fortunately, my mom made an appointment and met with the principal. She explained what was going on. He sat in on the classroom and saw my struggles. He then allowed me to do my assignments with my left hand and observed me do them successfully, albeit a little slower than the other students. When he had concluded his assessment, he directed the teacher to stop forcing me to use my right hand for things. Left handed was just fine. He passed me on to the fourth grade.

I do not have the coordination to do tasks right-handed. Pounding nails, writing, using eating utensils, are all relatively straightforward things that feel very awkward to do with my right hand. Dad did not have much patience with me growing up. It was difficult for him to try and teach me how to do something in a "hands-on" kind of way. I approached everything opposite; from how I held things, to the way my brain processed things. At least I did eventually learn to shoot a rifle and shotgun right handed, and cast a fishing pole the same way. This assimilation made doing those things with him easier as I became older, compared to when I was younger. Hunting and fishing were his passions. With me being able to hold a gun at least the same way as him, he felt like he could teach me, instruct me, and I was able to improve progressively. That made us both feel better about doing those things together.

I never recall hearing Dad tell me that he loved me growing up. Not even once. There were times that he had made broad statements of "You kids know that your mother and I love you." There wasn't a time that he had conveyed that to me personally in a father/son kind of chat. In fact, the first time he made it personal was in his letters that he wrote to me when I was in basic training. He had taken to ending his letters with "Love, Dad". I about fell off my foot locker the first time I read it! We never spoke about it, but I took to ending mine the same way.

I was out for wrestling, cross country, and track, which he had no interest in supporting. He made no bones about not finding any merit in athletics or team sports. He was a pretty good pool player. I bought an aluminum pool cue from the Gamble's hardware store, and my sister sewed me a custom case for it. I was shooting pool regularly in the Empire Cue & Café when I was in junior high. By high school, I was frequently entering pool tournaments on Saturdays in local bars. I was often winning trophies. Competing in billiards competitions seemed to gain some of my dad's long desired favor.

I wasn't a saint in high school, but I was still connected to my church family, out for sports, getting good grades in school, and working as a stock boy at a local grocery store. I also worked as a skate guard at the local roller skating rink. The skate guards got to skate for free, and the owner spent time giving us skating lessons to learn jumps, spins, and how to dance on skates. Mom loved roller skating, and we were able to get her out to the rink sometimes. The roller skating rink became a place for making happy memories. The couple that owned the skating rink were believers in Christ and saw the business as a ministry for reaching out to the children in town. Many of the kids that frequented the skating rink, or their accompanying café and pool hall, were from families like mine. We were the at-risk-kids of our time, growing up in homes suffering through alcoholism and familial abuses.

One of the waitresses that worked in the café below the skating rink was married and had a young son. She and her husband moved into a house across the street from us when the older couple that had the farm had passed away. Her dad bought the little acreage and moved her into the house. She and Mom hit it off right away. Mom was babysitting her son for her. He hung out with us most of the time. She and her husband bowled on a couple's league, and they got my folks involved, too. It provided a lot of good fun and entertainment for all of them. They were a younger couple, and my parents had been through the worst of their struggles. My parents liked being able to help them and spend time with them. I even became a substitute on the bowling league with them.

Shooting pool at the roller rink did not offer the same atmosphere as the bars. The tavern offered the chance to play in a tournament, win a trophy, or spend a buck to try and get control of the table for the night. By high school, I spent more time playing pool in the bars than in the safe atmosphere of the roller rink. I experimented with drinking alcohol. It was a small town and the taverns also served as gathering places for people. They were little neighborhood gathering places. The bar owners knew me, knew my dad and knew other relatives of mine. It seemed like an expected "coming of age" thing for a teenage boy to be in the tavern, sneaking a few drinks, and shooting pool. That's how it felt to me. The older pool players had taken me in and liked me. I responded to their instruction and teaching me how to shoot. Billiards, eight balls, nine balls, three balls; it did not matter the game. I was learning it all, and getting pretty good at it. So good in fact, that in a few more years, the local tavern team I played for would win our league championship, followed by the 1st place in our division. We took 2nd place in the Midwest Pocket Billiard's Association (MPBA) finals in 1980-81.[25] The older guys that mentored me in the tavern when I was a kid knew their game.

When I was slipping into the bars to shoot pool, I was sixteen years old. I was kind of responsible for a teenager. My folks gave me a lot of autonomy to go where I wanted and to do what I wanted. I could hang out with the friends that I wanted to spend time with about anytime. Let's face it. My parents didn't know how to raise teenagers. To them, being a teenager meant that you should

---

[25] I shot for "Hoot's Saloon". MPBA officials held the tournament in Dubuque, Iowa. We earned a spot to the Nationals in Las Vegas, but most team members were unable to go so we canceled.

be old enough to take charge of your life. Looking at it through their lenses, that's how it was for them. As long as I kept it between the lines, they allowed me that kind of freedom. Pretty typical of small towns across the country, my friends and I also experienced drinking at keg parties, going to wedding dances, and listening to bands at ballrooms. These were gatherings of family and friends, and drinking was a part of the culture.

Dad knew almost all of the bar owners, and sometimes I could talk him into entering a pool tournament with me. He was aware of the older guys that were mentoring me on the game. Some of them were known as hustlers in his days of slipping into the bars as a kid. And, they liked to brag to him about how good I was getting at the game. One of the guys was somewhat of a trick shot artist, and he taught me a couple of easier tricks to master. Even today, I can usually execute them flawlessly, turning heads in a family den or around a bar table for friendly competition. Like hunting and fishing, getting good at billiards seemed to gain some favor with my dad and draw us closer. Nonetheless, I was already on that slippery slope that would lead me down my prodigal path for a few years.

On one of my summer breaks in high school, I was allowed to go in a semi for a cross country trip. Dad had a friend that drove a semi over the road. Dad made some extra money servicing the trucks for some independent drivers. He told Dad that he could use the company, and someone to keep him awake. He asked if I could go with him on a run to the east coast. My dad agreed. I was excited because it meant seeing other states; adventure; and feeling somewhat independent. Dad would have never allowed my older sister to do something like this. It almost became a coming of age experience for me.

I was at a truck stop on the east coast; drinking and acting like a big shot. My dad's buddy talked a local prostitute into approaching me for sex. She told me that he had already paid her for it. She took my hand and went to lead me to the truck. I was scared; felt awkward; anxious; I chickened out. I couldn't have sex with her. My dad's buddy gave me a hard time about it; me not being ready to be a man; that kind of junk. My dad heard about it when we got back. My dad, as far as I know, never got upset with his buddy. Dad never challenged what he had done. He just laughed and shook his head as if he was confused and couldn't understand it either? She was a lovely woman. I wanted to have sex. I couldn't follow through with it. I was scared; confused; conflicted. Now, with the response of my dad and his buddy, I felt like there was something wrong with me. I felt like I should have had sex with her. I think that experience influenced later decisions that I made with prostitutes in the towns outside military bases. I am not blaming them. I am not angry at them. I'm trying to put the pieces of my life together and understand the impact it had.

I had already met with a recruiter and broke the news to my folks that I wanted to enlist in the Marine Corps. Since I was still a juvenile, my mom initially refused to sign the papers. Reluctantly, she agreed to sign. However, in the event I was called up for overseas duty she claimed she would invoke her "sole surviving son" right,[26] and she would keep me stateside if it took contacting a Congressman. At the moment, that was good enough for me! Let's fight one battle with her at a time! As far as my dad, I think he had a mixture of emotions. Doubt that I would be able to survive basic training. Fear that I would embarrass him by being sent home without graduating from boot camp. To some extent, the pride that I wanted to follow in his footsteps and serve in the Marines. I am sure that he thought it would toughen me up and make me a man.

I know today, the most compelling reason that I enlisted in the Marines was to prove something to him. When I graduated from boot camp, he would have to admit that I did measure up. Then, I could feel like he finally accepted me, wanted me, and maybe even loved me. He had never come to any of my athletic meets; no wrestling tournament, track meet, or cross country meet. I don't recall him even asking about them.

He was excited when I got a job at a local grocery store at sixteen. I had already disappointed him when he had gotten me a job at thirteen years old working at the local dry cleaners. It was my job to clean out the machines. The owner was a friend of my dad's through a veteran's organization, and he was doubtful about me being able to handle it at my age. However, my father had convinced him that I could. With a reservation, he gave me a try. Although I put my best foot forward, mechanical skills were not my strong suit. They were my dad's. Enough said. I did not have the dry cleaners job long.

I disappointed him over a decision to quit the grocery store job my senior year. The manager was not able to work my schedule around wrestling. He told me I would have to choose. I had wrestled since an intramural grade

---

[26] Reportedly named after the Sullivan brothers from Iowa who all lost their lives in WWII

school program. The elementary gym teacher ran the intramural program. He was another man that was a mentor for me. He was always so encouraging and positive. When I finished the 5th Grade Intramural wrestling tournament with a 4th place ribbon, he was as excited as I was. And, he already was saying encouraging things about 6th Grade! I enrolled the next year, and won my first blue ribbon in anything! The date was April 1st, 1970. When I got out to the car, I was so excited to show my mom the 1st place ribbon! She was even excited and gave me a big hug! She told me my dad would be proud of me, too. Unfortunately, though, that just wasn't the relationship that we had at the time. He was more interested in who I had to beat to get 1st place. Since they were not considered feisty boys either, it didn't matter so much to him.

I was a pretty chubby kid at the time. My weight class was 110-120 lbs. in 6th grade. I was one of the heavyweights. Although I was a premature baby, my growing up years were a roller coaster of fat to slim; back and forth. That trend would plague me all of my life. Even when I would slim down and lose weight, I still carried my fat around my middle. So, I was still chubby.

In our practice drills to learn moves and holds, one of the stellar wrestlers in a lighter weight class would often laugh and say, "I'll take the fat kid." He could roll me up in knots, just like a pretzel! He was stronger, faster, and more self- assured. He went into a family-owned business as an adult, and I came back to my hometown twenty years later and purchased something from him. We shared laughs about it then. Even though I was the "fat kid" on the team, he pushed me to try harder. He encouraged me never to quit. He was a grade ahead of me in school. He chose other sports over wrestling in high school, but he still took the time to come up to me and apologize for making fun of me for being the fat kid. He encouraged me to stay involved with wrestling and sports. When he had the humility to come up to me and apologize, I was blown away. It was one of the first times I felt accepted and felt like I might just fit in somewhere after all.

Although I was only a mediocre wrestler, I loved the sport! In junior high, though, I was seeking my dad's approval more than anything. I did not go out for wrestling in 7th-8th grades. I joined the team again in high school. My dad hunted and trapped. There was a dual purpose. Wild game was a staple of our diet growing up, and the fur trade was another way to make extra money. I had an interest in hunting and trapping, too. I thought if I would do more of the things he enjoyed, it might help me get his approval. He and I continued to struggle with our relationship. Although we did have some fun hunting and checking traps, the support I was searching for never actually came. Some of the guys on the wrestling team encouraged me to come back out for the sport in high school, my best friend and his cousin being two of them.

Our moms' named us after each other; a promise made while they were both expecting. My best friend's cousin was an exceptional athlete and well-liked by everyone. Besides wrestling, I learned to play tennis from him. The city park had a band shelter for outdoor performances. I batted tennis balls into the back wall of the shelter to learn to play. Tennis was popular, and I spent some lawn mowing money to buy a Spalding racquet at the local hardware store. He came up to the band shelter one day and joined me. Then, he invited me down to the courts to play. He was a part of the in-crowd at school. I felt accepted. He taught me the rules of tennis and how actually to play. He introduced me to his friends, most excellent athletes. We often played tennis until late at night. Another tennis buddy and I would even shovel the snow off the court in the winter to play. I found something I was becoming good at for a change. Some of these guys also wrestled and took to mentoring me on the grappling mats, too. I fitted in with people. I was glad I made the decision to go back out for wrestling. Most of my yearbook scribblings also make reference to my tennis abilities and expected future in the game. Not surprising, I still play, and have enjoyed passing this recreation down to my sons.

I was always a junior varsity wrestler, second string squad. But, the camaraderie with the other guys and the coaches was something I had not experienced before. My high school coaches had me pumped that my senior year was going to be my year. I quit the grocery store job to wrestle. I figured I was going to the Marines after graduation, and I had a lifetime to work. Wrong answer! My dad was livid! He did not speak to me for weeks, other than to tell me how wrong I was. To make matters worse, I broke my collarbone in a wrestle off for a varsity weight class spot. Yep, you guessed it. Wrestling ended for the season.

Now, Dad was all about the "I told you so" and how stupid I was to quit the grocery store to wrestle. Fortunately, the family physician thought that I still had plenty of time for the collarbone to heal before I had to take my last physical, swear in the official oath, and ship out for basic training. My life had seemed to be one disaster after another of disappointing him. I wasn't tough enough; wasn't smart enough; wasn't skilled enough. Going off to join the

Marines seemed like the last chance I had to earn his favor. On a positive note, though, I made the yearbook listed as a varsity wrestler at a weight class that I never got to wrestle at that year! Coach asked me if I would become the team manager after the injury, so I was still a part of the team.

Our Head Coach was a former wrestler for the University of Iowa, and their college athletes and coaches shared a wrestling banquet with us my senior year. Iowa's new Head Coach was an Olympian. The dinner was spectacular! Just meeting the U of I Wrestling Team, let alone talking to him, was every wrestler's dream. What stuck out to me the most, though, was the way the college wrestlers were willing to get to know us. They asked us about ourselves. They gave us wrestling tips and encouragement. One of the college wrestlers to share some words of encouragement with me went on to win a national title, world title and made the Olympic team. Those are the kind of events that give a boy hope, and a desire never to quit chasing his dreams.

A buddy of mine sparked my interest in wrestling again when we were stationed in Japan at the Marine Corps Air Station (MCAS) in 1977. The base was putting together an intramural wrestling team to travel and compete with other military bases. He convinced me to go through the tryouts and give it a shot. I knew I wasn't a good wrestler, but a boy has got to dream, right? We hit the gym and practice mats! My time as a grappler in the Marines was short-lived, though. In practice, I reinjured my collarbone. I was back in an upper body clavicle brace. The Navy Corpsmen thought it a good idea for me to give up wrestling before it resulted in an injury requiring surgery, pins, and reconstruction.

God always has a way of seeing plans come to fruition, though. Years later, as a youth counselor at a boy's home with troubled youth, some of them had an interest in wrestling, and they needed a coach. I was back in business! I was able to use some skills and knowledge of the sport to coach other boys. This gift would surface again when my youngest stepson took an interest in wrestling in an intramural program in elementary school. I talked to the coach and offered to be a volunteer assistant with him. The coach promoted the wrestling program as a father/son kind of bonding experience. He welcomed my assistance for the season. Although my stepson only went out for wrestling that one season, we had fun! I was newly in his life, and it helped to grow a strong bond between us that still exists today.

I need to get back to the Marines and taking the prodigal son path. The Native American Cherokee parable reminds me of the two wolves and the grandfather trying to help the grandson understand the conflict going on inside of him. Much like the Apostle Paul describing man's inner conflict in Romans Chapter 7, I had my war raging inside of me between the flesh and the fruits of the Spirit. At different times, I fed the evil wolf more than the right wolf. In that year I served overseas, I would achieve one of my greatest accomplishments, as well as face one of my biggest trials.

I had learned the best of both worlds from my dad, the respectable and the malevolent. In my mind, I was trying to play these out on a grand stage. The two wolves fighting within me collided. Unfortunately, it was not the last collision with life changing consequences. I was a stellar Marine. I had earned a meritorious promotion. I received a Meritorious Mast award, one of my highest honors. I had excellent proficiency & conduct marks. Regrettably, I also began to feed the evil side more. I was regularly drinking. I was getting into some bar fights over the two most common vices, hustling pool, and jealousy over a woman.

I did not like to fight in school. I tried to walk away. On two occasions, my dad was so furious with me for backing down that he drove me back uptown. We found the other boys, and he tried to make me fight. Fortunately, his acting like a lunatic caused them to scatter and the fight never happened on those nights. I simply went home embarrassed and humiliated. My real disposition as a young boy was being shy, timid, and lacking in self-assuredness. I was passive. I was pretty introverted. I didn't have a lot of confidence. I was a sweet boy. As I got older, I gained confidence in some areas compared to when I was younger. I became more extroverted as a teenager, compared to when I was a boy. I was still somewhat shy. I went from being a sweet boy, to a good man. But, I was beginning to believe the adage, "Nice guys finish last."

When stationed in North Carolina for supply school, I was brutally assaulted by three other Marines. It was late at night, and very few taxis were still working. To catch a ride back to the base main gate was about 15-20 miles away. I told these guys that I would split the cab fare with them. I would pay half the fare, and they would only need to pay the other half between all three of them. They agreed, and we all jumped into the cab.

At the road to the main gate, the taxi driver pulled over to let us out. It was still about a two-mile walk to the gate. I paid him my half of the fare; $15. The other guys refused to pay and got out of the cab. I told him he would have to collect from them. They jumped me outside the cab. The driver drove off. There was no one to help me. I fought the best I could, but it didn't take long for me to go unconscious. It got cold at night. A Marine guard on patrol happened to see my body lying in the ditch alongside the road when the headlights of his jeep dipped a bit with a depression in the road.

He got me to the base infirmary. I woke up to the big lights overhead in an emergency room. The attending doctor was examining my injuries. I reportedly had a fractured jaw, broken nose, and damaged eardrum, along with numerous bruises and contusions. The doctor said that had I laid out there all night; I could have died from exposure and hypothermia. I knew two of the Marines that had assaulted me. There was an investigation and report filed. They were located a short time later and confessed to the attack. I was in pain, physically and emotionally. I was angry. I had righteous indignation. I did not want to fight. I wanted to walk to the base gate, slip into the barracks, and go to sleep. Looking back, I should have simply paid the rest of the cab fare. I am an idealist, though. I had honored my part of the agreement. I wasn't expecting to get assaulted.

It brought back high school memories of being beaten up and bullied by a couple of different guys. Being too scared to fight them. Trying to flee. Coming home to deal with my dad being angry because I refused to stand up for myself. Having him order me into the car to go back to town to settle the fight. Nice guys finished last! Cowards never won! A switch was thrown within me that night. I swore that I would never be beaten like that again; ever. My dad had two favorite sayings when I was growing up, "I may not always be right, but I am never wrong." And, "If somebody wants to fight, you fight. They might get a meal, but at least you'll get a sandwich." I was ready to collect on some overdue meals and sandwiches. I would still walk away when I could; when I was allowed to. However, I had become hyper-vigilant. Now, if I sensed a fight was coming, I struck first; fast and hard. If that was enough edge to give me an escape route, I still took it. I mostly just wanted out of the situation without getting hurt.

Besides adding fights to my extra-curricular activities, I had taken to the occasional visiting of local prostitutes in the bars outside the base. It was easy to rationalize overseas because these were women that worked in the nightclubs as waitresses and companions. When someone had spent enough money in the bar to make it profitable, he might be invited to be her guest for the night, and maybe asked to move in and help her share some of her expenses. Some of the women were looking for a ticket to the states. Some were simply doing what they had to do to earn a living and survive. The further I slipped into the abyss, though, I found my way down the dimly lit back alleys of the town, into the real red light district, where the women could no longer sell themselves in the nightclubs on the main streets. As much as I had slipped into ugly depravity, I tried to convince myself that it wasn't anything that was out of the ordinary. I knew the truth, though. After each encounter, I walked back to base feeling guilty, dirty, and ashamed.

A group of us had taken to lounging outside the enlisted club swimming pool on hot days during the summer. We would drink, swim, and show off as we did different dives off the boards. Not wanting to be "bested" by any of the guys, I climbed the ladder to the high dive and was set to make one more swan dive out across the sky and hit the water like a torpedo! The guys were calling me down. They were concerned because I had too much to drink and my balance was off. I chose not to listen, waving them off. The next thing I knew; I was floating on the surface of the water which had turned blood red. A couple of my buddies dove in and were pulling me from the pool, telling me I was going to be okay. Someone was yelling for a base ambulance. I was loaded onboard, and taken to the base hospital. Unbeknown to me, I had misjudged my spring from the diving board and catapulted myself into the shallow end of the pool. I thought that I had plenty of clearance to strike the water, dive deep and then turn back up to the surface. I only had about 3-4 feet of water. My head hit the bottom of the pool with significant force. Besides splitting my head open with a pretty good size gash, the doctors took x-rays and told me that I was one very lucky Marine. I had only compressed some of the vertebrae in my neck and back. Years later, a doctor in Cedar Rapids would look at his set of x-rays and call them compressed fractures, now scarred over.

I had continued to feed the evil wolf within me. The wolf prone to pride, ego, jealousy, envy, inferiority; and now it had caught up with me. My supply lieutenant showed up at the hospital and said, "Damn, son, what are you trying to do, kill yourself?" He wrote a personal letter to my folks explaining that I had been in an accident and was expected to make a recovery, although my status in the Marines was yet to be determined. This diving accident was the first of two major wake-up calls for me concerning this juncture of which wolf I would continue to feed. I panicked and thought I would be put out on a medical discharge. I had to be able to perform all of my duties and pass my physical fitness tests. I begged him to give me a chance to prove that I would recover and could do everything expected of me. I told him about my dad being a combat Marine in Korea. I said that I could not get sent home under a medical discharge. I was still months away from being deployed back to the states. He agreed to delay any permanent decisions. I had my chance! As long as I could perform my duties at the supply depot and pass a physical fitness test before deployment, he would support me staying on active duty. Fortunately, the injuries were not as severe as initially feared, and the lieutenant assured me I could stay in the Marine Corps.

Recovery wasn't easy, but God had sent me a personal trainer, a woman Marine that was a sergeant. She and I had become acquaintances at chow hall and chapel. We walked to the commissary together. A platonic friendship not mired by complications of sex. She was public about her faith. I needed a trainer, and she volunteered. We walked. We talked. We shared stories about our hometowns and families.

Walking returned to running. The base was bordered by a massive sea wall that we often ran on. It was very freeing to jog the wall. I was back to feeding the right wolf and not his evil twin. I was able to perform all duties and pass a physical fitness test within standards. Not quite as glowing of marks as previous, but passing. That was all that mattered. When I deployed back to stateside duty, I was probably in the best shape of my life holistically. Mind, body, and spirit seemed to be all connected again. I was looking forward to coming back home on a short leave before reporting to my next duty station.

Figure 13: Dad overseas; circa, 1953; {{PD-USGov-Military-Marines}}

Figure 14: Me overseas; 1977; {{PD-USGov-Military-Marines}}

Figure 15: Me on desert deployment, 1978-79; my weight was a problem for me in the Marines, too. After this deployment, I was put in an individual fitness platoon.

Figure 16: Holiday Season, January 1978; back from overseas duty.

CHAPTER TEN:

Coming Home

I returned to stateside duty in late December of 1977; able to spend the holiday season with family and friends. A lot had happened in that year I was overseas. My older sister had birthed her first son. My next younger sister had married her high school sweetheart, who joined the Army after his graduation. Grandma Nellie was adjusting to life without Grandpa Louie. It was her second Christmas without him. She surrounded herself with family and stayed busy all of the time. She was especially excited to be a great-grandma. My older sister and the baby lived with her for a time until getting out on their own.

Mom was about the happiest I ever recalled seeing her. It was the second Christmas since she had lost her mom, Grandma Sylvia. The last years of her life, she had lingered in a nursing home. It is hard to make the trip to visit; about every other week or so. She had succumbed to multiple strokes, and death was a blessing. The first Christmas was the hardest. Not only was Grandma gone, but I had shipped out for overseas duty; something that my mom had sworn she would never allow happening. She worried about me always. My younger sisters told me that when Mom got the letter from the lieutenant about my diving accident, there was non-stop crying for days. Dad finally told her there wasn't anything she could do about it 6,000 miles away. It was going to work out however it was.

Christmas of '77 she was a Grandma of her own. Her first grandchild! And, her son had made it home from overseas safe and sound! Her next younger child was newly married to an upstanding young man in the Army. She still lived at home until arrangements could be made for her to join him in Germany. Mom's youngest was still in high school, and in many ways, she had become her closest confidant. Mom also had her coffee club friends in the neighborhood that she visited with daily.

My youngest sister had a pack of girls she ran around with that was crazy, fun-loving, adventurous spirits! If you could think of it, they could imagine it. And, they would try it! A mother of one of the girls was a strong woman of faith. God put it on her heart to shepherd these girls. She started a weekly bible study with them. This mother kept them connected to the right sides of their nature. She was their rock in times of trouble. She was an eternal optimist. She knew how to love unconditionally. My mom was grateful for this connection that her youngest daughter had made.

In addition to all of that, Dad had been sober for quite a while. He gave up alcohol for coffee. They made new friends. They kindled some old friendships with other couples that left their tavern days in the past, too. This period was probably the happiest they had been since starting out on their own. They purchased a travel trailer camper in the Spring and spent much of their time camping with friends. Dad had taken up trout fishing, which he loved with a passion! In the winter, they would often be at the homes of those friends having coffee, visiting, playing cards, and planning the next camping season. Mother hen had all of her chicks around her, and the man sitting beside her transformed into the kind of husband, father, and grandfather that she knew he always could be. It was a very merry Christmas after all.

I had gained some favor in his eyes, too. From basic training in San Diego to a Fleet Marine Force (FMF) tour that took me to Japan & Korea, I had retraced some of his earliest footprints in the Marines. Now, we could share stories about our military experiences together. He was interested in my overseas tour of duty. Especially, how much Japan and Korea had changed since he had been there. I felt like I was proving myself to him. The Christmas leave in '77 gave me hope that I was beginning to measure up into the son that he had always wanted. The legend of him that I had created in my mind did not seem so aloof.

I wanted to feel close to him and have the father/son relationship that had been a fleeting thing (at best) growing up. I told my folks that I would rather buy a car and drive down to the base than board a bus or plane. I wanted transportation while I was stationed there, anyway. And, I could drive back home on occasion with authorized leave. My newly acquired brother-in-law's Dad was selling his '74 Mustang II. Candy-apple red, with a white vinyl top;

sweet little car! I bought the car and planned the road trip to South Carolina. I had an assignment to a Marine Corps air station in a small town called Beaufort.

Dad loved country music, especially all of the old stars enshrined in the Grand 'Ole Opry and Country Music Hall of Fame. He had never been to Nashville. It was on the direct route for driving to my next duty station. I suggested to Dad that if he assisted me with the driving, we could stop off in Nashville for a few days and see some of the sights. Once we arrived in Beaufort, I would send him home on the bus. Surprisingly, he agreed. The Mustang had a set of studded snow tires that got us on the road, and we were off! We got into Nashville some twelve hours later.

We stowed our gear in a hotel and set out to see the lights and sights of the big city. We visited Ernst Tubb's Record Shop and the famous Tootsie's Orchid Lounge downtown on Broadway. Dad had always fancied himself a singer. All of my life growing up, he had played the part of wearing fancy western shirts, cowboy boots, and western belt buckles. Now, here he was at world famous Tootsie's Bar. Whomever the band was that played that night, they were picking away at some old country song that he knew, and he convinced them to let him stand up there next to the mic and sing along for a verse. He was feeling pretty special! Truth told; so was I. Both of us were sober. Drinking sodas and coffee, and having the time of our lives together. We took in the Ryman Auditorium and the Country Music Hall of Fame the next day.

We made one more road trip like that when I came back home for a visit in the Fall of '78. We stopped off in Nashville to take in the recently opened Opryland. I had met a beautiful Southern Belle and asked her to marry me. I was not quite 20 years old, and she was all of seventeen and in her senior year of high school. Her father, in some ways, was a lot like my dad. He had been a sergeant in the Marines. He had also loved his time in the military and wanted to make it a career. However, his wife had grown tired of being a Marine's wife, and they eventually settled down in a little town outside of Beaufort, S.C., called Burton. That was her home. She grew up there. Most of her family still lived there. Like my dad, he was a skilled mechanic. He had opened an auto garage in town.

That's where I met their daughter. Her family welcomed me in and adopted me as one of their own; especially her grandmother, Nannie. I loved her telling stories and eating pecans on the front porch. And, I enjoyed the large family gatherings they would have. They didn't seem to be afflicted with all of the dysfunction and chaos that I had grown up with in my family. There appears to be love, caring, and fellowship between all of them, the immediate and extended family.

I still gave in to the evil wolf from time to time and went out drinking with my buddies. Nothing usually too reckless, other than hustling on the pool tables for a few bucks. As luck would have it, though, the night before my first date with Nannie's granddaughter, I was in a fight with another Marine. He was angry about losing money to me on the pool table. I tried to avoid the fight, but he jumped me in the parking lot outside the bar. I showed up at her door wearing big sunglasses to cover up the black eye.

Her Dad, Mom, sisters, and Nannie were all there. She wanted me to meet her entire family. Her Dad lifted the sunglasses and looked at my eye. He gently lowered them down and calmly stated, "Son, if you think you are going to date my daughter there are at least three rules; no drinking, no bars, and no fighting; period."

Fortunately, I had been coming into his auto garage for a while and was friends with his chief mechanic, Lee. Both being former Marines, they knew what the lifestyle could be like in the military. Her Dad made it clear that he wanted more for his daughter, though. I promised him that I would abide by his terms if he let his daughter still go out on the date. We were going out for dinner and a movie. It was a double date with her girlfriend. Any concerns that her family had quickly quieted. Throughout the next several months, I stayed true to my word. When I wasn't on duty on base, I was spending all of my time with my girlfriend and her family.

I was in love. I'd never felt this way about a girl (woman) before. I had crushes on girls in high school. I had the experience of puppy love and going steady. I had gone to homecomings and proms. I left for the Marines without having a steady girlfriend back home. So far, my experiences with grown women had not been about being in love. I lost my virginity through an affair with a lady unhappily married at the time. There were a few women over the next couple of years that I dated; women I had casual sex with at times. And, of course, the prostitutes overseas. My experiences with sex were nothing to be proud of for a young man. I was ashamed. I felt dirty. I was one hot mess when it came to sex and relationships.

There were two women that I dated overseas that I never had sex with, a Japanese woman and a Korean lady. One was a college student from Hiroshima, Japan, and the other worked in a family jewelry store in Osan, (city) Korea. By dating these two women it allowed me to feel like that boy in high school, again. Dating was fun! It was sometimes scary, but in a good way, though. It was clean. It was fresh. It was innocent. I didn't want sex to contaminate it. It felt the same way when I met Nannie's granddaughter. She was clean. She was fresh. She was innocent. She was fun. She wanted to remain pure until her wedding night. I agreed. I didn't want sex to contaminate our engagement. When we were finally intimate, I wanted it to be making love; something I had never experienced before.

As fate would have it, though, as her high school graduation got closer, my promise ring gave her pause to consider her life. She realized that she was so young! I was the first boy she had ever dated. The idea of getting married suddenly scared her to death! By now, her family had taken me in as their own. I was already considered family. But, she had to follow her heart. She called off the engagement. Not only that, she stopped dating me. She started dating someone else. Although I was hurt and confused for a while, now as I look back, it was the right thing. The other man she started dating married her. She was ready for marriage and a family. Her family took him in as well. They have remained together for all of these many years raising their family together. God is good. Amen.

I was not handling it so well at the time, though. I was not as accepting then. I had not grown up. I was not ready to put childish things aside.[27] She was my first love. I had even agreed to get out of the Marines and live in South Carolina. I wanted to start a family with her. I had been so excited about the engagement, I came home and shared the news with my folks and sisters. I convinced Dad to take another trip south to meet her and this beautiful family that had taken me into their fold. The break-up was not only hard for me but hard for her family at the time. They had accepted me and planned for me to become one of their own. After the breakup, her family remained friends with me. Until her Grandma Nannie's passing, we wrote and corresponded often. I did take a trip back down to visit, too, before Nannie died. Her older sister stayed in touch with me for many years even after Nannie was gone.

---

[27] I Corinthians 13:11 references putting childish ways away when we grow up.

The turmoil of the broken engagement, combined with the loss of Lee, her Dad's mechanic, was the catalyst that gave me another excuse to feed the evil wolf. Lee had recently separated from active duty and was working for her Dad at the auto garage. Lee was from Alliance, Nebraska. We had made a pact that when I separated from active duty to come home to Iowa, he would go with me to show me the West. Alliance is cowboy country; close to Wyoming and the Black Hills of South Dakota. We never made that trip together. Lee had died from an accidental electrocution before my enlistment expired. Over thirty years later, I tried to find his grave but was unsuccessful. My choice to pray at the Veteran's Memorial in the cemetery was all I could do.

With Nannie's permission, Lee boarded a horse at her acreage. Although the animal was tame enough to ride, the horse did not like the confines of being fenced into the field. The horse often got out, and Lee would hold a roundup to get him corralled again. Lee decided his only alternative was to get rid of the animal or install an electric fence. Nannie gave him permission to install the fence, even though no one else had the love for the horse that Lee had. On the day that he was a stringing fence, Lee was supposed to wait for me and another buddy of mine from the supply depot to come out and join him. Lee did not wait for us to get there. He started without us. My buddy had gotten there before me and saw the accident. The wind whipped the electric fence up into a powerline that arced. The current traveled down the electric fence, through Lee, and blew out the heel of his cowboy boot, as the current grounded into the earth. I heard the siren as I was pulling into the farm drive. The ambulance had arrived at about the same time as me. Someone told me it was Lee laying in the field; that he was hurt. I ran across the field. Plowed ground, I think? I remember it was uneven; hard to run. It was too late. I was too late. Attempts to resuscitate Lee failed. First responders had tried. We watched Lee get loaded into the ambulance. He was declared dead after arrival at the hospital. In a relatively short period, I had lost a fiancé and a close friend.

Up till then, the only other death that difficult for me was my Grandma Sylvia's. She meant the world to me. I took care of her after the Colonel died, staying with her over the summers until she had a stroke and could not live alone. We moved her into our home briefly, but it was too much for Mom to handle. Besides, we had no room in that little house. Grandma had a pull out bed in the middle of our living room. Mom placed her into a nursing home.

She had more strokes, and died before I graduated from high school; April 1st, 1976. I wish it had only been an April Fool's joke, and not the cold, hard, truth.

She loved me; cared for me; was interested in me, and was concerned about my life. She wondered what I would become, at least until her strokes and declining health disabled her. In her last days at the nursing home, mine was the voice she still recognized. I was who she still responded to with an acknowledgment of knowing me. In my mind, all I wanted was for her to see me graduate from high school and join the Marines. But, for some reason, God was punishing me (my thoughts at the time) and He allowed her to die about a month before I graduated. I was angry at God. I was grieving the loss of someone that I knew loved me more than my parents did.

Now, two years later, I was feeling that same way all over again. I was angry at God. Why did He have to take Lee? Why couldn't my fiancé and I stay together and get married? Why did He hate me so! Why didn't God want me to be happy? I decided to rebel, again. The evil wolf wanted to feed. I was full of self-pity. I allowed bitterness to consume me.

I was at odds with some of the guys at the supply depot. Aside from hanging out at the barracks with a few guys, most of them weren't my friends. I didn't feel like I had many friends besides my ex-fiancé's family. To make matters worse, I had been passed up for promotion to sergeant. I had more than enough time in grade as a corporal. I still had good proficiency & conduct marks. Supposedly, the senior staff sergeant and supply lieutenant had run the paperwork up to S-1 (Administration) recommending the promotion. However, the sergeant major had called me over and told me quite candidly that he did not think I had earned the promotion, yet. The paperwork was not leaving his desk until he decided it would. Whether it was real or imagined, it was my perception that other sergeants' in the supply unit were colluding to block my promotion. There wasn't any love lost between us, let's put it that way. But, a corporal has got to know his place; especially when in the presence of someone holding another stripe on their sleeve. Regrettably, I would learn that lesson the hard way.

CHAPTER ELEVEN:

The Roaring Lion

W here were my grandfathers to warn me about the two wolves, or to read from Peter's gospel in chapter 5, and remind me, "Be on your guard and stay awake? Your enemy, the devil, is like a roaring lion, sneaking around to find someone to attack."[28] They were gone. To make a collect call home was a burden on my folks. They did not have the extra money. And, my dad had been experiencing some health problems eerily like his father's; cramping and weakening within his legs. He was seeing doctors at the Veteran's Administration Hospital and trying to get it figured out without any real luck. They were confident from muscle biopsies that he did have some neuromuscular problem that was probably genetic. Not only had his father been crippled, but so had his aunt and another uncle. Unfortunately, fear of doctors and hospitals was very real in my grandfather's generation. None of them ever sought a diagnosis until my Grandpa was nearing his death. He agreed to allow doctors at the U of I hospitals to take tests. Although doctors told him for years that it probably was multiple sclerosis, the doctors now ruled that out and confirmed that he had some muscular dystrophy. The doctors explained that there were many strains of the disease. I don't know that they ever conclusively identified his.

My dad needed canes and crutches to walk around. For a short while, he wasn't able to work. He couldn't handle the pressures of standing on the concrete floor of a factory for long hours. A friend owned a service station in

---

[28] I Peter, Chapter 5:8 (CEV)

town and offered my dad a job pumping gas. He could work as much or little as he felt he could handle. And, if he felt up to it he could do some light mechanic work like fixing flat tires and oil changes, all with the ease of hydraulics'. When no one was on the drive for gas, he could sit on a stool and give his legs a rest. We were all worried, though. We had grown up with Grandpa crippled. We watched the Jerry Lewis Telethon and knew the realities of having muscular dystrophy. Eventually, these kinds of diseases would take someone's life. How much time someone had did depend on so many variables yet unknown at that point. Each disease progressed at its pace.

So, on top of my issues that I was back to drinking again over, I worried about my dad and his health. Within a short period, I had managed to alienate myself from other personnel in my unit and the supply depot. Of course, everyone except the drinkers and partiers that had grown to hate the Marine Corps, and who could not wait to separate from active duty. Drinking and partying to escape reality became the norm. My feelings of persecution within the supply depot only grew. The bitterness and contempt must have shown. Most days were not pleasant for me or anyone else in my vicinity. I was back to the sins of the flesh; drinking too much; bar fights as a result of hustling pool, and affairs with unhappily married women.

Even the sergeants' that I was convinced despised me took notice that I was deeply troubled. They knew about my marriage engagement that had ended, and about my friend dying. They didn't know anything about my dad's situation, though. They were men a few years older than me. They married and had children. From the stories they shared, they had grown up with tough times of their own as urban youth. We were from different cultures; different ethnicity; had little in common, but we all knew pain when it surfaced. I knew they meant well expressing to me that "there's more fish in the sea, so get fishing." They told me that I would find the right woman someday, and in the meantime, just have fun dating; just be patient.

They even expressed some sincere regret at the loss of my friend and related some of their experiences with death. They tried to get me to focus on the good times with Lee, and if he had survived the electrocution, he probably would not have been the same person. So, it was a blessing for him to die. Looking back, I can honestly see that they meant well. The lack of having a positive relationship with them, though, left me guarded. I was always wondering if I could trust them. I wasn't quite convinced that the caring was real.

On paydays, there was a tradition of "Bosses Night" at the enlisted club. It was an excuse for some drinks and camaraderie after securing the supply depot. The sergeants' and some other Marines that I was sure wanted little to do with me invited me along. But, it meant some free drinks, and that happened to be something I was doing a lot of most days. The more beers and drinks I had, the more I allowed my insecurities to become public. I climbed on to a "pity party" and began to share the struggles that my dad was having back home and that I was worried about him. After all, he was also a fellow Marine; Korean War vet and all. A man who was only in his early forties and wondering if he would ever walk again without a cane? Remember the reference about the devil being a roaring lion that never sleeps and seeks to destroy?[29] I wish I had read that bible passage that day! I was not alert, and Satan was on the prowl.

One of my nemesis sergeants' leaned across the table and interrupted me from feeling sorry for myself with the comment, "F*ck your 'old man!" The results were not good A physical altercation ensued. Fortunately, it was quickly contained by the others present. My behavior was threatening. The sergeant told me to get control of myself; I was already responsible for an assault. The trap had been set, and I stepped into the snare. By morning, other superiors were aware of the incident. The commander sent word with a time for me to report to his office. I was never disciplined or sanctioned, no black marks or blemishes in my service record book (SRB). And, now I had cooked my goose! As I was waiting outside in the hall, the sergeant in question exited from the commander's office. Oh, great! I couldn't imagine anything good coming from that! Was there even a point to me telling my side of the sorted story?

The commander was a lieutenant colonel. The Lt. Colonel was a former ground command officer assigned to the air wing. The chief had seen some stuff back in the day. Although he had graying hair and some semblance to a grandfatherly type, he was still not a man to be trifled with over anything. He was a tough commander with grit. He did not ask me for my side of the altercation. Why should he? A Marine that outranked me made a verbal remark that I did not like, and I physically assaulted him. Case closed. I was

---

[29] I Peter, Chapter 5: 8-9; the message about Satan as the roaring lion paraphrased.

guilty. No further evidence needed. The commander expressed concern about my drinking, my associates, and my recent behavior. The commander only told me in practical terms, what he would do. Send me to the Brig to discharge my active duty from there, or send me to the naval hospital at Charleston for a new drug & alcohol treatment program. He told me the choice was mine. I chose Charleston. He went on to say that the sergeant had requested to speak with him, also. He explained that the sergeant had told him about his remark and that he intended to provoke a fight. The sergeant told the commander that if there were disciplinary proceedings to follow, he should be punished, too. The man that I was certain despised me went to the commanding officer on my behalf to request granting me mercy. I began to see the sergeant and his friends in a different light. I knew that the sergeant involved, as well as all of the sergeants at the supply depot, cared about me and the problems I had with them were because of me. I was an emotional, physical, and spiritual wreck. None of them were out to get me.

I went to Charleston to complete the initial phase of the treatment program. Phase two was returning to base and working with the counselors for the remainder of my enlistment. The Commander wanted to keep me under closer watch, too, so he sent word to the supply sergeant to temporarily reassign me as needed. I was often called out for temporary assignment to be a duty driver for the commander or as transport back and forth to Marine Corps Recruit Depot (MCRD) at Parris Island. Periodically, there were Marines from the unit that would get into some trouble and get sanctioned for it with a short hitch in the brig. I would be responsible for picking them up and transporting them back to the base.

Whether planned or sheer coincidence, one of the guys I transported back to the unit was assigned to be my roommate in the barracks. Although it was awkward at first for both of us, we eventually, to some degree, became friends. At least, we became friendly towards one another. I performed the transport duties with a sense of humility. I knew all too well that I should have faced the same fate as some of these men for similar actions. Was that part of the commander's plan? Some penance for me to serve?

I worked with the captain and lieutenant that had oversight of the outpatient substance abuse program the remainder of my active duty enlistment. Not surprising, these were men of faith that lived it publicly. Something the captain would often say still sticks with me today; "Corporal

Cole, your mind is like a computer. If you feed garbage into it, you're going to get garbage out of it. Do you want to succeed? Then, pay attention to what it is that you feed into your brain." Years later, when introduced to the concepts of cognitive-behavioral therapy, it was like sitting down with the captain in his office. I guess he was a thinker ahead of his time. And, the lieutenant would remind me of the importance of not putting human limits on God. Relying on Him for my strength and getting through each day. He also helped me realize that I was a fallible human being. That what I did, right or wrong, did not define me. I was a child of the Creator.

I was back to Chapel; back to Bible study; back home with my Father (God). Like the prodigal son in Jesus' parable, the sins of the past did not matter. God welcomed me back.[30] I went to my first 12 Step meeting at the air station. I made friends with Marines that took care of themselves mentally and physically. Getting secured from duty meant a trip to the mess hall followed by night in the gym. When I did go out with friends, some of them drank only water and the ones that drank alcohol were social drinkers that would have one or two and switch over to soda or water. One of the guys wrestled on the U.S.M.C. wrestling team. He deployed to wrestling competitions across the globe. I met him at the barracks when he came back from the match. He befriended me and invited me into his inner circle of friends. He knew a lot of the locals, too. I was getting back to normal. Like who I was when I was connected and in right relationship with God.

When I separated from active duty in June of '79, there was a going away party in the commander's office. In addition to the substance abuse program, he had ordered me to participate in the company's fitness program. I had months of daily running, weight training, exercises, calisthenics, and weekly weigh-ins. Besides the other consequences of the drinking and partying lifestyle, I had packed on the pounds and gotten "sloppy" in uniform. When I discharged, I had lost about thirty pounds! I looked fit! I felt great! I was once again a sharply dressed Marine! I was so happy when the commander pinned a good conduct medal on my chest. He shook my hand, and told me that he was proud of me! He even had a military photographer there to take a few pictures.

---

[30] Luke, Chapter 15: 11-32; "Parable of the Lost Son"; a story of a son rejecting his Father and coming back home.

His smile and firm handshake said it all. Now it was time to come home and face the demons of my childhood.

CHAPTER TWELVE:

Storm on the Horizon

I came home from active duty feeling great! I had two years of "ready reserve" status. I was only called up once to report for active duty to the 4th Marine Division in New Orleans. However, before the date to report on the orders, the active duty status was rescinded.

Looking back, I can see that there were some adjustment problems that I had with the return to civilian life. Although I had not served in combat, the world has never been at peace. There have always been countries fighting internally, or with each other, and American politicians and military leaders were deciding that we had to be ready to protect our interests. There were times we had simulated training exercises and readiness drills. Even readiness drills can sometimes become life-threatening and result in casualties. Being in a combat supply unit providing support, there wasn't much chance of that happening to me, but this was certainly a concern of mine for Marines serving in other units. These exercises and drills took on an entirely different meaning during overseas duty.

A couple of incidents that stand out is when the Army officers were killed in the demilitarized zone (DMZ) border between North and South Korea while trimming trees in August 1976. I was in final phases of basic training and about to graduate boot camp. We were alerted to the incident, prepared for possible deployment. It turned out to be just preparation and readiness drills. Drill instructors had initially told us we were going to Korea, though, whether that was true or not. The alert status rescinded, we went to graduation from basic training with our respective orders for schooling as usual. I was assigned to supply school in Camp Lejeune, North Carolina. I graduated top of my class and got to choose my next duty station of the bases available. I wanted a tour in the Fleet Marine Force (FMF) with duty at the Marine Corps Air Station (MCAS) in Japan. FMF commitment originated in Camp Pendleton, California, with deployment to the West Pacific duty station designated.

I was pretty excited about following in my dad's footsteps. He had also gone through basic training in San Diego to mechanic school at Camp Lejeune, to Camp Pendleton and deployment to FMF in Japan. From there, he was deployed to Korea at the end of the conflict in 1953. As a kid, I was excited about looking through his photo albums, especially pictures of Japan and Korea. I was fascinated with how different the cultures looked from ours in America. I wanted to experience the open markets, rice patties, narrow village streets. I wanted to meet the people; see the landscape, especially Mount Fuji. I wanted to walk through the beautiful temples and shrines in Kyoto, Nara, and Tokyo. And, I was determined to get to Korea somehow! I was on a mission.

About halfway through the overseas deployment to Japan, we were alerted to an incident, again. This time, an Army helicopter had crashed. It was July 1977. We were told that the aircraft had been shot down by North Korea for reportedly crossing DMZ air space. Fortunately, the incident was resolved peacefully. At some point on that overseas duty, we did a comprehensive embarkation and deployment exercise. It was around this time frame. Embarkation and deployment readiness became a primary focus. Another helicopter had crashed earlier, in March 1977, as well as a plane in July 1977, due to adverse weather conditions. These incidents create tension as investigations occur to sort out details. I worked in combat supply; Marine Corps Property (MCP). We were told the comprehensive exercise was a real alert and not just a training. Within 24-48 hours we had combat gear loaded on pallets, boarded transport planes, and sat on the flight line ready to deploy. We played cards, talked about home, and wondered what we were about to experience when those planes landed. We would not find out. At that point, we were told it was a readiness drill to assess deployment preparedness.

Although only readiness drills and simulated exercises, it speaks to the heightened sense of duty and security in an overseas arena. Even back then, there were hot spots with skirmishes occurring all over the globe. Our base was also an air station that housed fighter jets and an occasional reconnaissance plane. Flight line and hangar guard duty were taken very serious. Any breach of security protocol would lead to being disciplined. Guard duty, base security, and combat readiness were all at a different level than on stateside duty, at least looking through the lenses of an eighteen-year-old Marine at his first real duty station; a Fleet Marine Force (FMF) command. I was willing to serve in the fighting, albeit in a rear support capacity supplying combat gear. I know I should just be grateful that God shielded me from that. It's hard to explain. I am grateful, especially seeing the young military personnel coming home from Iraq and Afghanistan engagements with their struggles. I just have a personal issue with the comments made about only being a "peace time" Marine.

That was the term given to us that served in between official engagements. Like we were somehow less than other Marines? I was ready to deploy on the combat alerts and drills. I served on guard duty overseas and protected planes, flight lines, armory, and provided base security. We dealt with the nationalists and their anti-base sentiment, demonstrations, and protests to express their disdain for our continued presence there. Saigon had just fallen to the communist North on April 30th, 1975, ending the Vietnam War (The Learning Network, 2012). There was still unrest in multiple regions of the world. I served with Marines that had been in Vietnam and served in that era. The possibility of another engagement somewhere was real. Going from peace time to combat can happen quickly.

Please don't misunderstand. I am not comparing my experiences to those of combat Marines or other combat service personnel. Some of them gave the ultimate sacrifice for our freedoms. Many others have lasting wounds, both physical and mental, as they work to heal from their horrible ordeals. I would never disrespect them by comparing my service experiences to theirs. I am saying that there aren't any "peacetime Marines."

The globe has always had places of unrest. We didn't get up every day at the sound of reveille, feeling like it was another day at boy scout camp with a list of merit badges to earn. At least in overseas commands, we were always at the ready; constant vigilance and alert; assessing situations and incidents occurring around us. At times, we were led to believe a warning was real. I think in some of those situations, commanders were reviewing intelligence, correspondence, and making decisions moment by moment that could have quickly gone from a readiness alert drill to active engagement. We were doing our part to serve and protect. No, not combat. But, not boy scout camp, either. There's an adjustment when someone returns from habituation in that environment. That's all I'm trying to say.

My father had issues with his adjustment to civilian life. He also appeared to have some traits of PTSD. His violence was very explosive. It was extreme. It seemed to come without warning. And he drank heavy to escape or numb the pain of something. He talked quite a bit about his military experience, except while in Korea. He was there at the end of the conflict. The only specific incident that he ever disclosed was about picking up bodies of Marines that had stepped on a mine. He cried. His voice cracked. His hands trembled talking about it. He only shared that with me after I had already enlisted. Then there is the Colonel. His wounds were so severe that he was hospitalized for an extended period when he first returned. It's my belief that the adjustment issues returning from overseas military duty are on a continuum. It's not that they don't exist. More accurately, where are they at on the continuum? For some it will rank slightly; for others moderate; and others yet, severe. We don't help soldiers heal by denying that the adjustment problems exist, or for someone else to tell them how they should rank these things on their continuum. Many individual factors influence their ranking.

It's not unlike surviving sexual abuse. Sometimes the obvious isn't obvious. I remember a girl in treatment that was gang raped by some high school boys. The girl was recovering well from that. The girl knew she wasn't at fault since she had no relationship with the offenders. The issue she was emotionally stuck on in treatment was another disclosure she had shared. About three years earlier when she was just entering puberty, her Dad kissed her and put his tongue in her mouth in a sexual way. A sexualized kiss was a severe violation of what fathers are supposed to do to their daughters. Then, he told her it was their secret.

Maybe we should get better at encouraging clients to disclose to us what their emotional problems and adjustment issues are, without deciding for them what should be the least or the worst? Isn't it better if they rank the issues, and then tell us? Then, we can try to put an effective treatment plan together with them. Maybe we should consider this approach with our veteran's, too?

The soldiers of my grandfather's era were put in hospital wards to recover from physical wounds, but the depth of their mental and emotional wounds were not understood. My dad had no physical injuries. He returned to port in San Diego, and the 1st Marine Division marched the 38 miles to Camp Pendleton; no ticker tape parades; no ceremonies; no real acknowledgment of what they had endured. It was called a "police action" by our administration;

not even a war. Merely a declared conflict. No treaty was signed declaring peace; just a cease-fire agreement with a fortified demilitarized zone on either side that has continued to see fighting. No wonder the Korean Conflict has been aptly called the "Forgotten War." (Hynes, 2013)

How much of my grandfather and father's post-traumatic stress and adjustment issues were attributable to combat and military experiences is debatable? I never served in a combat arena; merely an overseas duty, readiness drills, alerts, assessing daily security threats, and simulated deployments. We all have symptoms of post-traumatic stress disorder. Sebastian Junger, in his work "Tribe: On Homecoming and Belonging", actually found that the chances of suffering from chronic PTSD were more directly related to the soldier's experiences *before* enlisting in the military, rather than their actual military experience. (Junger, 2016) Junger goes on to state that military service can have positive effects on soldiers coming from dysfunctional families. Serving together with other soldiers creates healthy bonds and attachments, and promotes a sense of comfort and security. The other common bond uniting my grandfather, father, and me beyond our military service is experiencing some form of familial abuse or dysfunction in childhood before ever joining the military. That's true with my grandfather having been abandoned and placed in an orphanage for six years. At least the indications of that are present within my father's family of origin. I know that it is true for me. My experiences with familial abuse before enlisting in the military are more responsible than anything for my own symptoms of PTSD.

I did finally make it to Korea on a temporary assignment of my own. The supply lieutenant knew how important it was to me. I had told him about my dad serving there as a Marine. A couple of other assignments had not panned out, but he said, "Cole, don't worry. I'll get you over there to Korea on an assignment before you have to rotate back to the states." He was always trying to get guys to extend their overseas deployment, adding there was a better chance for more travels and temporary assignments. He offered, but I politely declined. He was true to his word, though, and I eventually got the assignment.

He routinely would secure temporary duty assignment (TDA) for guys in the supply depot to get some rest & relaxation (R & R) while picking up something from another supply depot in a neighboring base or serving on a West Pacific deployment. One sergeant went to the Philippines and Australia. Some us took short hops to Okinawa. And, some went to the air force base south of Osan (City), South Korea, where there was a big supply depot. The lieutenant sent me to Osan on a short R & R leave assignment. At orientation, we were briefed on base security and protocols for leave and liberty. We were told that a North Korean patrol had infiltrated into South Korea in the past, as recent as last year. To someone new to the base, it seemed like security was elevated. That was probably only my perception at the time since we were able to leave the base and go into the city. However, concerns were still present, if talking to local Airmen was any indication. They still spoke of the incident and the potential threat of it happening again. Airmen only informed me of this for my safety while I was there.

Seeing the villages and cities were a pretty humbling experience, also. South Korea was not as technological and industrial as Japan. The country was still pretty poverty ridden. When I secured off base liberty and went into the town to see the sights, I was fascinated. There was at least one orphanage in the village outside the base. During the daytime hours, the children would carry shoe shine kits and ask to shine shoes for a buck. I bought food, candy, and little toys and gave these to the kids. One young boy followed me back to the gates of the base. He had his toy and was smiling. I had somebody snap a picture of him with my camera. I still have it in an album somewhere. Sadly, some of these kids had servicemen as fathers that had deployed back stateside.

Many of the women worked in the clubs and were involved in prostitution to survive. They weren't able to take care of the children, either. Thank God for the orphanage and those healers willing to work there. At least someone was giving those kids faith, hope, and love. Coming back to duty stateside was a huge adjustment. The villages directly outside the base gate catered to the evil wolf within every serviceman. Feeding the lusts of the flesh without regard for the collateral damages and residual consequences left behind. In my view, soldiers, Marines such as me, became habituated to a distorted picture of reality. To some extent, we thought we were entitled to anything whenever we wanted it. People, particularly women, were there to serve our physical needs directly, and they liked and enjoyed it. Now, I can sadly see that it was only a matter of survival for them. They were doing what they must.

After spending an overseas tour of duty in villages across Asia artificially fabricated for our pleasures, it created a warped view of many things. It's not real. It's not how the real people of those cultures live. It's not a real typical village in Japan, Korea, or any other country. Ask any serviceman. You have to get miles away from the bases actually to begin to experience a country and the pure culture. The world directly outside the gate is a creation of others to market to servicemen. Whatever want, need, desire you have, it can be bought. It is certainly not like small towns across America. It wasn't like my hometown.

At least for me, some adjustment issues carried over into stateside duty, followed by separation from active duty to civilian life. I'm not blaming the military for that. I'm not accusing the villagers that were only making a living however they could. I'm saying, I wasn't prepared for it. I should have been. My father had photo albums of his overseas military tour. Albums are full of pictures of companion women, bars, clubs. Fantasizing about it, and the reality of experiencing it is often different. Rather than feeling like a man, it left a part of me broken; hollow, and riddled with shame knowing I contributed to their objectification.

The first chapter of James goes into a detailed discussion of who is responsible when we give into our evil desires, and we are dragged away by temptation.[31] I am responsible. It was my fault for my behavior. I chose to give in to the temptations of the artificially created playgrounds outside the bases. No one forced me. No one made me. I knew the truth. I had accepted a relationship with Christ as a teenager. I turned away. I chose to feed the evil wolf. Periodically, I would still feed the respectable wolf, so he did not starve. I had times I was sober. Times I did not seek out companion women. I visited beautiful authentic villages, like Kin Tai; a small mountain village that had an incredible cherry blossom festival in the spring. It was nothing like the community directly outside the base. Everything was different, the people, the atmosphere, the environment.

I met a beautiful Japanese woman there. This woman was a college student. We had a platonic friendship that was beautiful; pure; innocent; fun. We talked about wanting more, but this woman could never leave her family in Japan, and I could never stay. We loved each other or at least I thought I was in love at the time. And, I refused to be selfish and ruin it by pushing her into a sexual relationship. I couldn't do that to her. I couldn't hurt her that way.

---

[31] James, Chapter 1:2-16 is a commentary about our responsibility for the sin that dwells within us.

It was similar to a Korean woman I met in the village outside of the air base at Osan. She worked at a family jewelry store. We had a similar relationship. She could never see herself leaving Korea. I knew I couldn't stay there. I was on a short temporary assignment. I never pressured her for sex. These platonic friendships were beautiful expressions of caring, if not love. I'm glad it never got complicated with sex. I had no idea about how to have a healthy committed relationship at that time. Especially a healthy relationship that also involved sexual intimacy. I would have damaged them both. I'm glad God did not allow that to happen.

Author's note: As I wrote this particular chapter, I became very unsettled. I know God used it to speak to my heart. When people ask me about my military service, most ask if I served in combat. I tell them "No", but I always qualify that we were alerted to incidents that had us "at the ready." For years I have taken issue with being called a "peace time" Marine. I should embrace the title with humility and gratitude. I never fully appreciated the fact that those engagements ended peacefully, and spared me and others from the horrors of war. Being a combat Marine was not my destiny. God's plan for me was to become a criminal justice professional serving public safety here at home.

CHAPTER THIRTEEN:

The Storm is Here

I grew up with a Marine for a dad, so his brand of structure and discipline was apparent. However, I also think he had fears of my older sister blowing the lid off the sexual abuse and telling someone about it. He was afraid of her telling me about the sexual abuse, especially as we became older teenagers, compared to when we were younger, and he had more control. He still had more control of my sisters than me, and he knew it. Looking back, I think a lot of the autonomy and freedom given me was because he was aware that I had my love/hate relationship going with him. If he were leaving me alone, I would not make any waves about the problems between he and my older sister.

The biggest confusion for us as siblings was that we did not understand the extra dimension to the love/hate relationship that my older sister had with Mom and Dad. That confusion was enhanced as she got into high school and was entering her senior year. I was a sophomore. It was self-serving for me not to understand it, so I didn't question it much. I had practically unlimited freedom and autonomy. She, on the other hand, had virtually none. And, she was older. My dad kept her on a tight leash for what seemed like all of the right reasons.

"She's a girl. She can't take care of herself as a boy can. There are so much more things that can happen to her than to a boy." These were common explanations given for her restrictions. There were loud family arguments with my older sister screaming at my parents that they let me do everything, and she got to do nothing. My father was a master of control as he would calmly lay out all the rational, logical reasons restricting her from doing certain things; overnights with friends, school dances; dating. He had finally given me some rest. Most of the time, I was off of his radar. I somehow knew that it was conditional, though, based on the freedoms and privileges he granted me. Back then, life was a matter of survival and taking the path of least resistance. I was not going to "poke the bear."

Our younger sisters did not understand much of any of it. They knew that their Dad drank too much when they were little and one time hit Mommy, but he was sorry. And, life was better now. I was playing out my role of getting along. They didn't understand why our older sister wasn't. She became viewed as the problem. She was the one that needed just to let go of the past and move on. Dad was different now. Why couldn't she just forgive him? And, the anger she had toward our mom was totally coming from left field for all of us? The rest of us saw Mom as a victim of his drunken years, too. My older sister seemed even angrier at her than at him. That made no sense to us?

As these arguments escalated, my older sister would scream that she couldn't wait to get away from home! She couldn't wait to go off to college. As the next older sibling, I thought that if she would just ease up, Dad would back off. My younger siblings thought if she could just leave for college, life at home would get better; immediately! She was sitting on the one family secret that none of us could fathom. At this point as siblings, we were all still clueless. We had not connected the final dot to the dysfunctional love/hate triangle that existed. She tried to tell us in the only way that she could. She would only scream that none of us understood! She would have tears streaming down her face and shout, "If the rest of you kids only knew what was going on!"

Dad took that as his cue to stop any further discussion. When he said a discussion was over, none of us wanted to push him further on it. We knew there was something different going on between them; but what? Couldn't we figure it out? What Dad sexually abuses his daughter? Children can't even create that image. Emotionally, I could feel and sense her pain. I just couldn't understand it. It couldn't be physical. I got the brunt of that, uncensored from others. Corporal punishment was on public display within the family. It was only private outside the inner circle. I knew there was a different dynamic at work for her, but my mind was shielding me from having to face it.

She had been an above average student in high school. Made the honor roll. She was a teacher's pet. She often brought homework for them and helped them with organizing assignments, papers, grading and special projects for their classes. All the teachers loved her. My older sister was smarter than me.

She was more talented than me. My older sister's life had so much more promise for success than my life did. Her high school teachers had helped her with her applications and preparation for college. They were as excited as she was when she got her acceptance letter from the University of Northern Iowa (UNI). Her time at UNI would be short-lived, however. On the surface, it looked like her life did a complete 180-degree turn. She was unraveling. She was coming apart at the seams. She was spiraling out of control. She was spending too much time drinking, partying, and some of her grades were failing. School officials gave her notice about a student aid reduction. Our parents told her they would not help her with college expenses, and she needed to come back home to work. She dropped out of school with plans to re-enroll within the next semester. She never returned to college. After a brief stay in an apartment, she lived with Grandma Nellie, who was a widow and would welcome the company. She was always fondest of my older sister, much like Grandma Sylvia was of me.

My dad blamed the campus minister. My sister had gotten connected with a Bible study on campus. It was the one bright spot for her while in college. She and the minister had become close friends. My dad's twisted spin on their relationship was to accuse him of being an older man that was only preying on poor, innocent, naïve college girls. He implied that there had been some illicit affair between them. In reality, the campus minister was the first person my sister felt she could trust to share her secret; her father had been sexually abusing her since she was a 12-13- year-old girl.

When I returned home from the military, there was still lots of confusion about our family dynamics. Things were better with family members. We were on a journey of healing. Like with the Hebrew people wandering in the desert following their exodus from Egypt, we would spend a few more years living in the wilderness before entering the promised land.

My older sister had an apartment in town and lived with her baby boy. She and the father of the child are never married. She was a single Mom. My nephew's birth father was a Navy veteran that was a few years older than me. We used to shoot pool in the bars and drink together. I don't know that I would have called him a friend so much as a bar-room buddy. He played on our relationship enough to charm my older sister into bed. He had no desire to marry her or become a father. He just was looking for sex and a good time. I remember how excited she was when she told me in a letter that they had met at one of the uptown bars, and he talked so much about me and how proud he was of me to go off and join the Marines. He had been a Sailor. The Navy and the Marines are of the same brotherhood when they want to claim each other. She talked about him being funny, and that she had finally met a nice guy that cared about her. I had my doubts just knowing him. And, I was feeling guilty. She was so excited to tell me that she was dating a friend of mine. A good man. Having my approval meant a lot to her. When she told him she was pregnant, he wanted no part of it and no more to do with her.

When I returned home from active duty, my older sister wanted to tell me her secret. She couldn't, though. She was afraid of what I would do. Dad and I were mending fences, but my feelings of rage were right under the surface at a constant boil. I was still trying to live in his shadow. He had lined up a job for me at the battery plant where he had worked. I was worried that the job wouldn't be a good fit for me. I should have told him that I didn't want the job, but I was afraid of making him mad.

He was a hard worker. He contained his alcoholism pretty well through the years. He would have been called a functional alcoholic. He never missed work. He would do the job of two or three men and never complain. His employers had wished they had ten of him. His endorsement of me meant something to them. I went through a quick interview, but the foreman made it clear that he intended to hire me, and that he was expecting to have another "Bud" at the plant. I should have learned from the past. I had my strong work ethic. But, I did not have the same skill set as my dad or share his desire to work in the factories on assembly lines. I do admire the people that can do it. God bless them! We need them! They are some of the hardest workers I have ever known. It simply wasn't me.

It didn't take long, and the personnel manager called me in to discuss not keeping up with the assembly line. My hands and arms were raw from a reaction to the glue used to seal the grid plates into the battery cases. My doctor had even written a letter recommending transfer to another job. I'd worked in supply and warehousing in the Marines. I knew shipping & receiving, inventory control, running a forklift, and all of the associated tasks. I requested a transfer to the warehouse. He told me there weren't any openings and tried to convince me to hang in there until something opened up. Chances were slim, though. I had no seniority. Warehouse jobs were considered premium. For a few more weeks I tried wearing long gloves and made a prop use to push the grids down into the cases. It didn't help. I still had a reaction to the glue touching my skin, and using the prop slowed me down even more. I knew it wasn't going to work out for me, or for them. I quit the job.

Once again I had disappointed my dad. Not only had I damaged my reputation, but I had also tarnished his. He took it personally. I had embarrassed him; shamed him. Mending fences with my Dad over the hurts of the past was over. I crawled back into my pity party and a bottle. I returned to feeding the evil wolf. All of those childhood wounds laid bare again. I had punched a self-destruct mode into overdrive this time, though. The next few months were a blur of heavy drinking, keg parties, bar fights, and building a reputation for being a "badass" Marine. I'd taken a construction job working for a drinking buddy that needed an extra man. The work didn't involve a lot of technical skills or mechanical aptitude. Mostly a lot of lifting, hammering, and pounding. I had also completed a metalworking and welding course in the military. Those skills worked out nice for my boss. He had a lot of scrap metal and old farm machinery that he needed cut up for salvage. Much of my job was cleaning up the aesthetics of the farm yard. We worked hard. We drank hard. And, as for me, I hustled a few dollars on the pool tables, hit the dance halls, and took to running with some guys that liked to fight occasionally. I guess we were all trying to prove something to ourselves, or somebody, back then.

It was a pretty common occurrence that my dad would drive up to my youngest sister's house and inquire about whether she had seen me or not. Her home was my haven. She is where I sought rest and escape. She would casually reply, "Nope. I haven't seen him. Why?" Even if I was inside sleeping it off. My dad would matter-of-fact state, "Well. When you see him tell him, the police are looking for him. He needs to stop into the station and see what they want. Better than them having to pick him up."

I would stop at the police station the next day and talk to one of the officers. They all knew me from high school. I wasn't a troublemaker for them. I think the officers knew I was having some adjustment issues. Most of them liked me. When they would show up at a fight, I was polite, cooperative, answered their questions, and followed their directives. Most of the time, they were looking for one of the other guys I had been running around with, anyway.

A couple of occasions, I lost control of my car and hit utility poles. Fortunately, I was never charged with a drunk driving offense (not that I didn't deserve it!). I paid fines for simple misdemeanors and traffic citations because I had either driven away or abandoned the car. When I reported to the police for questioning, I was always sober. Police charged me with leaving the scene of an accident and failure to maintain control. A couple of the local officers pulled me aside and counseled me, though. They were firm and direct. If I did not get control of myself, eventually something was going to happen that would have serious consequences.

One night, after being in a fight, I staggered home to my folks. When I got there, I decided that I was going to walk back uptown and finish the fight. I had woken my dad up, and he stood between me and the front storm door. He gently put the palm of his hand on my shoulder and said, "Rand,' why don't you go back and lay down. Go to sleep. Nothing good is going to come from this." I was for lack of better words, a hot mess. My life was out of control. I wasn't taking any responsibility for it. I was blaming my dad for all of the childhood pain, and I was angry. No, not mad; resentful. For feeling like I never measured up to him. I was never good enough. Never aggressive enough. Never the son he wanted. As a kid, I hated fighting. I avoided fighting. I couldn't please him then because I refused to fight. Now, I had my reputation of being wild, a little crazy, and willing to fight anybody that pushed that envelope with me. You'd think he'd be happy? I'd turned out just like him. One problem, though. He had changed. We were out of sync; out of time with one another. Neither of us was happy.

All the feelings of inferiority, resentment, and rage erupted. I shoved him hard right through the front storm door. He and the door ended up on the front lawn. Before he could get to his feet, I had pounced on him. I jerked him to his feet and said, "C'mon old man! Let's do this! I'm not a little boy anymore! You will never kick my ass again!" I thought we would finally have the showdown that was long overdue. I stepped back and prepared for his assault. In my head, an F-5 tornado had just touched down and was going to unleash all of the furies that had been pent up inside me for years about this man. The storm was here! And, I wasn't running from it this time; I was creating it.

He was in his early forties. A little weaker than his prime, but not much. The neuromuscular problems with his legs had gone into remission. He was back working full-time in a machine shop hoisting heavy steel. The Dad that I grew up with would never have tolerated what I had just done. Dad was forty-three years old at the time of the lawn incident. He wasn't old. Dad wasn't afraid of me. He wasn't afraid to fight. My father had been a fighter. He was a bare knuckle boxer on the loading docks. All that I had heard about from men in the factories, and experienced myself growing up, was his fast, hard, hands.

I remember a backyard gathering, and my friends and I were doing wrestling takedowns and typical "dominant buck" kind of behavior. I was in high school. My dad decided that he was going to take me down. I think his plan was twofold; embarrass me in front of my friends, and also put me in my place. I seized on a surprising move and executed a successful takedown. The look on his face said it all. He was glaring at me! I was stunned. I never expected that I would "best" him. I let him up, and he was dusting himself off from the dirt and grass. Some of his friends were crowing about "Rand' just got the best of his old man". I knew this was not going to end well.

Unwittingly, I had embarrassed my dad in front of his friends. He played it off as letting me take him down. He even laughed and shook my hand in congratulatory fashion like we had finished a real match. The look on his face said it all, though. He wasn't happy. He didn't like getting bested by anyone at anything. I was waiting for the other shoe to fall. I just didn't know when.

I had some friends that boxed at the local boxing club, and I had been asking my dad about letting me join. I did some sparring with them on some Saturdays in the city park. One of the guys was on the cross country team with me, and we ran together for workouts. He had a brother that boxed, too, and he would run down past my place and pick me up to do some road work with him. It's hard to explain. I didn't like to street fight. I walked away from guys even after being knocked down. Multiple times. I was an athlete, though. I liked sports. I loved competition. I enjoyed watching boxing on ABC's "Wide World of Sports" or coverage of Olympic boxing. I read books about some of the boxing greats. To me, it wasn't fighting. Boxing was just another sport like wrestling.

Shortly after the backyard wrestling takedown incident, there came a Saturday that Dad and I were home alone. He asked me if I still wanted to learn to box. He told me he would teach me how to fight. The city dump was just south of our place, and there were lots of treasures I had rescued. I had some old boxing gloves I had found. I put them on, and we "sparred". He clocked me. Hard blows, one drew blood from my mouth; another from my inner left ear. Let's just say it hurt. He wasn't wearing gloves. I know that he was initially concerned that he might have hurt me. When he saw that I was fine, he let me know that he just needed to put me in my place. Standing in the bathroom doorway, with me getting cleaned up, he gently slugged me in the shoulder like guys do to each other when bonding, and said, "You okay?" "Are you going to be all right?" What was I going to say? Cry and whine about it? Not hardly. I had agreed to the lesson.

I was expecting a repeat performance that night on the front lawn. But, the storm I envisioned never came. He truly wasn't the same man anymore. He steadied himself and started to cry a little even. At least his eyes were watery. His voice quavered a little. He gained his composure and said, "Rand,' you can hate me for your childhood. It was hell most of the time. I'm responsible for that. I can't change it, but I am sorry, whether you believe me or not. I am not going to fight with you. Not tonight. Not ever. Never again. I was wrong. I love you. I've changed. I'm sober now. I'm living a new life." He went on to say, "You're a grown man. I hope you will come back inside and get some sleep. We can talk more about this tomorrow. Just know that if you go back uptown tonight, whatever happens, it is your fault. You are responsible for it. It is not on me. Not this evening; not anymore."

With that, he climbed the front step, walked in the house, and closed the main entrance door. He just left me standing on the lawn, confused and looking at the mess I had made of my mom's broken storm door. There was no longer any fight in him, at least concerning me. That evil wolf was gone. He had starved it to death. But with me so unstable and angry, is it any wonder why my older sister was convinced that if she told me her secret of surviving his sexual abuse that I would probably have reacted with violence?

I upset my middle sister with the lawn incident. She was so angry with me. If not that night, then shortly after that, she was screaming at me! Crying. Telling me how selfish I was. She was angry that people put up with me acting that way. She yelled at me, "You're not my brother anymore! I don't have a brother. If anyone asks, I'll tell them that he's dead!"

My mom and my sister had the same fears. Dad had finally changed, and the family was getting rest from the chaos and turmoil. Everyone was finally experiencing some peace, except for me. There was a relief when Dad stopped drinking. The obvious abuses had stopped with the sobriety. No one knew about the hidden abuse of incest. Even that had ended about five years before this incident on the front lawn. The rest of the family was getting to a much better, healthier, and happier place. I was the one still stuck in the past. I was the one causing others in the family pain now. I was disrupting their lives. I was being selfish and not caring about how my actions were affecting them. The generational curse was continuing. It had now been handed down to me.

It took my middle sister about three years to speak to me again. My sister forgave me, but not until I had established a recovery of my own and proved that it was real. I realize today that it took courage for my sister to tell me those things that night. It was tough love. It was the truth. The brother she had grown up with had died. He was no longer around. And, she was fed up with the guy that had replaced him. Years later, she told me that she never stopped praying for me. She had friends in her church praying for me. We're very close now. We share our faith with each other often. We lean on each other for spiritual counsel and prayer. I'm convinced that only God can restore relationships like that.

CHAPTER FOURTEEN:

The Summit

The lawn incident with my dad took place in the fall of 1979. It was the best thing my dad could have said to me. Really, for the both of us. He needed to move away from the toxic shame of his past to a sense of healthy shame.[32] He was taking responsibility for his past, the harm caused by his actions, and he was working to restore the relationships. Although I wasn't ready to apply what he had said, it was good, Godly advice. In my heart, I knew it was the truth. I was responsible for my actions. Since I wasn't ready to hear it, though, I tried a geographic change to escape my problems.

I moved back to South Carolina for another new start. Mom and Dad both told me that I didn't have to go; I could stay home. They just didn't want to live in the past anymore. They had a real new life underway. They were happy. They had found peace. I felt like I couldn't stay. I felt ashamed for what I had done the night before. I told them it would be best for me to leave. I started my 1970 Ford Galaxy 500 and headed south. I looked in the rear view mirror as I pulled out of the lane and onto Brewer Street. Mom had gone into the house, while Dad stood out in the road watching me go. I think he must have been feeling like the father in the parable of the lost son who demanded his inheritance and left for another country.[33] It had to have broken my father's

---

[32] John Bradshaw, one of the foremost experts on healing from generational family shame describes the differences between toxic shame and healthy shame in his books and seminars

[33] Luke, Chapter 15: 11-32; "Parable of the Lost Son"; a story of a son rejecting his Father and coming back home.

heart. As I looked in the rearview mirror, I was angry and ashamed. I set my eyes back to the road and settled in for the long drive.

I moved in with a couple of buddies still serving in the Marine Corps, and I took a job at Hilton Head Island at a local resort community. It was an entry level position requiring some bookkeeping and supply skills; similar to what I had done in the military. Things were different, though. My friends and I didn't click. We didn't get along. It wasn't the same. The truth is; I wasn't the same. I had no peace. I had no joy. I was restless. Unsettled. And, I knew that traveling a thousand miles hadn't changed a thing. I could not run away from myself. I felt like the lost son. I wanted to come home, but my pride was stopping me from making the phone call.

After some time had passed, I called home to talk to my mom. I wanted to test the waters about coming back. I had caused a lot of pain before I left. I wasn't ready to talk to Dad. She said, "Just a minute. I'll put your father on the phone. He'll have to decide." I swallowed hard. Took a deep breath. My heart sunk. I was still feeling ashamed. I had not forgiven myself. I did not want to talk to him. But, I knew that I needed to.

When Dad answered the phone, I told him that I needed some help. I wanted to come home. He only said, "Do you need me to wire you any money?" I choked up. I told him, "No, Dad. I've been working. I've got money to come home. I'll see you in the next couple of days." Dad had previously introduced me to his friend, Bill, who was involved in Alcoholics Anonymous (A.A.). He was a spiritual man that had found his way back to God through A.A. and a 12 Step program. Bill & Dad had talked me into a voluntary committal to the substance abuse inpatient program at the Mental Health Institute (MHI) shortly after my first relapse after getting home. I was reluctant about the voluntary committal and was minimizing my relapse. I only stayed a few days and left against medical advice (AMA). Coming back to Iowa, I knew I needed to connect with the guys in A.A. again, and put a recovery together. I was running out of chances.

Once I got back, though, I was straddling the fence again. I had completed a substance abuse program in the military and had done very well for almost a year. I knew what I needed to do. At least I thought I did. I didn't want to go back into treatment. I went to 12 Step meetings with Bill, or Dad, or my sponsor almost nightly. My Sunday School teacher that was so influential in my life before called down to my dad's looking for me. He told me that he heard I was back in town. He wanted me to come back to work for him at the Model "A" Restoration garage he owned. My older sister and I had both worked for him for a while in high school. I needed a job. It was one that I knew; mostly shipping & receiving of car parts and inventory clerking. Those were skills I had. Skills I was pretty good at utilizing. And, he was someone that I knew cared about me. He was committed to his Christian faith. Being around him would encourage me to feed the right wolf and allow the fruits of the Spirit that the Apostle Paul describes in the New Testament to surface again.

I had usually gotten drunk on the heels of experiencing negative emotions. Alcohol abuse was a primary coping response to distress. Staying sober when I was happy, healthy, and feeling confident about life was not usually hard to do. But, I got complacent. I let my guard down. I became overconfident and began to coast. Things were going well. My dad and I were getting along great. We spent a lot of time at 12 Step meetings. He and Mom had their camping friends they spent time with who were all people I had grown up with, too. I often spent nights around the campfire with them, drinking coffee and joining in on some trout fishing. I was back to going to church with my boss and his family some of the time. That Baptist Church had been our refuge as kids. I went to weekly bible study with my youngest sister and her friends. I was dating once in a while. Things were looking up for me for a change!

One Saturday after work, I was invited to play in a euchre tournament in a tavern close to the auto garage. The tavern was also the only restaurant in the small town I worked in. We often would walk over at lunch to get food to carry-out and bring it back to the garage to eat. Some of the guys I knew asked me to get in on the tournament after work. I rationalized that I could drink soda. I liked playing cards. I'd grown up watching my grandparents and parents play cards. As kids, we frequently played euchre. I thought I could handle it. Mistake. Big mistake. Not ready. It was a relapse waiting to happen.

I went through a short stretch of on/off again drinking. I thought I could get it under control again, but I was eventually ticketed for failure to maintain control. I slid off the road on the ice and hit a light pole on the northwest side of town. The pole had a transformer box. When the car made contact, sparks flew, and the lid from the transformer box was catapulted into the air. The power in the neighborhood was knocked out. The car was still running and drivable. I put it in reverse, backed out over the curb that the car had jumped, and I left the scene.

This time, there was a witness, though. The man that lived in the nearest house had looked out when he heard the crash. He was about my dad's age. He had kids my age. He knew me and what kind of car that I drove. He called the police and made a report. My dad had a police dispatch scanner that constantly was on. He heard dispatch talking to authorities about the accident. He thought they were looking for me. He got dressed and drove to the police station. He was informed by the police that they wanted to question me. The officers investigating told Dad that if he could get me into headquarters within 24 hours or so, they wouldn't need to issue a warrant. He assured them he would locate me and bring me into the station.

His first stop was to my youngest sister's house. That's where I usually went to hide out and escape from my problems. This time, I wasn't there. I figured that would be the first place people would look to find me. The accident was up on Legion Hill. I had a buddy from high school that lived close. He was married and had small kids, but I was pretty sure he would let me stay for the night. I knocked on the door, and he answered. I told him I needed some floor space for the evening. He asked me what happened, so I gave him the reader's digest rundown. He laughed. Then he shook his head. He stepped out further to see that the hood and front grill were damaged. He said, "C'mon in."

I don't know if he called my dad or not after I finally passed out. The next day, my dad showed up at my friend's door, though. He didn't yell, but he didn't ask, either. He only told me, "Get in the truck. I'll take you to the police station to turn yourself in." I knew I couldn't run away from the consequences. I got in the truck, and we had a quiet ride downtown. The officer on duty put me in a holding cell. He'd known me since I was a kid. He had often stopped to talk to my friends and me when he was on patrol. Usually, when we were at the city park playing tennis late at night, hanging out at the skating rink, or fishing from the west side bridge.

After a while, he came back to get me. He said he had to fill out some paperwork. He asked me what happened. I told him that I lost control due to road conditions, my car jumped the curb, and I hit the pole. He wondered why I left the scene. I told him that I panicked; I was scared. He said there wasn't any point to asking me about whether or not I was drinking because he couldn't prove that I was drunk at the time of the accident. He told me that if I had reported it myself and came in on my own, he would have only charged me with the failure to maintain control. But now, he was going to have to cite me for leaving the scene of an accident as well. He told me the next time I wouldn't be so lucky.

He finished filling out his incident report. Then asked my dad if he should put me back in the holding cell until I could appear before the magistrate. I figured that was a no-brainer. Dad had always told me not to call him from jail; he wouldn't post my bail. He didn't answer the officer right away, so I think he was pondering the better lesson for me. The officer interjected that if I would sign a consent to delay initial appearance that he would release me to my dad's custody. Dad had to ensure that I appeared for my court date and paid the fine.

The longest I had spent in jail was an overnight at the provost marshal office in the military. I'd been detained on some other things, but always released without charges or citations. Dad drove me over to my friend's to get my car. I drove home and just wanted to sleep. Probably a dissociative thing, again. I didn't want to deal with things. Dad didn't say much to me that night. He told me that he, Bill, and my A.A. sponsors were there to help me, but they couldn't do it for me. My father said I needed to think about what I was doing and the friends I was running around with on a regular basis. He talked about me needing to change my friends and associates before I did something to mess my life up. What could I say? I just sat and listened. He was telling me the truth.

To my knowledge, there was only one Magistrate Judge in my county. She was a wise old Judge and knew the signs. It was also a small town and keeping your business private when drinking in public, never really worked out. I appeared before her as ordered and paid the fine. I wasn't expecting what she did next. She told her court reporter to stop transcribing for a moment. She decided to say something to me. The Judge took the time to lecture me sternly and let me know that she had a good idea about what was really going on. She told me that I better get myself checked into the substance abuse program at the state hospital voluntarily before things got worse and she saw me in her courtroom again.

I contacted my boss and asked him if I would still have my job in the garage when I got out of treatment. He told me that I would. I contacted my A.A. sponsor, and he drove me to MHI. He filled my folks in on what was going on. I checked into the treatment program. I listened. I applied myself. I completed the inpatient program successfully. I was assigned to an outpatient counselor for Aftercare.

The Magistrate had submitted a directive to the therapist at the inpatient program to inform her if I chose to leave against medical advice (AMA). I'm not sure who informed the Judge I was there. I had been in the program about six months earlier and refused to stay (released with an AMA discharge). The therapist convinced me that leaving the program on a premature release meant the Judge would issue a warrant for involuntary committal. I would be transferred to a residential halfway house program for six months to one year. True or not, I was a believer! The Judge and therapist now had my attention! In those days the substance abuse program at the state hospital was on a locked ward. They operated very similarly to a correctional institution. In a seemingly innocent situation, I refused to pour out my coffee when an orderly told me the resident lounge was closed. The orderly called for backup. In short order, multiple attendants physically transported me to a locked psych unit. I was responsible for it. I spouted off like I was some tough Marine and was belligerent. I was wrong. Call it an attitude adjustment. The transfer worked. In a few days, I was allowed to return to the substance abuse program. There were no more behavioral problems or outbursts from me. I did not want any more of the being locked up experience. I liked my freedom. I did not want to lose it. I knew that the Magistrate was right. I had already been given so many chances. There weren't any more left. If I messed this up, I had no one to blame but myself.

The outpatient counselor was great to work with when I got released. This woman was a cousin of my boss, and her parents also attended the Baptist Church that was so special to me. She had me completing a relapse prevention plan, emergency sobriety cards, emergency activity cards, and I had to carry a list of sponsors in my billfold with phone numbers. I had a reliable, stable recovery going for about three months. I cannot recall what the trigger was now, but I had a momentary lapse over something. There was some distressing incident. I bought a beer, opened it, and took a drink. I was immediately consumed with guilt. I was angry at myself. I knew that was not what I wanted to do. I threw it away. I drove up to her office and camped out on her steps all night. When she showed up in the morning, she didn't know what to think. I told her what had happened. She questioned me to confirm that I had not gotten drunk and in fact had the one drink and stopped. We processed whatever it was that had been the trigger, my feelings, and she explained what I did as a lapse versus a full-blown relapse. She was confident that I could get back on track with my sponsors and 12 Step program and did not need to go back to inpatient treatment. I was convinced that there was something I had missed in treatment. I didn't want this to spiral out of control. I told her I wanted to go back to the inpatient program, even if for only a few days to figure this out. She got it worked out, and my sponsor drove me back over. My boss was gracious and visited me to assure me I still had my job. But, he did have another guy working at the garage that did not have these problems. If I did not get it together, this time, he would need to give him more hours and let me go. Although he cared, he still had a business to run.

I cannot tell you today what that short stay did beyond tighten up my confidence to stay clean and work my recovery program. I wasn't there for more than a few days. It was two weeks at the most. When I left, my therapist asked me if I thought that I would be coming back again. I confidently told the therapist "no." I said that I had figured it out. I knew what I needed to do to keep from coming back.

That was the Spring of 1980. I've never gone back to inpatient treatment. I have spent select times as an adult referring myself to outpatient counseling and therapy to continue healing. I still needed to understand myself, understand my dysfunctional families, and to directly work with trained specialists that could help me grow. Not perfectly. Not without setbacks. Not without trials and struggles. But, I had reached the summit. I no longer felt like a victim of my childhood abuses. I was a survivor.

As John Bradshaw describes it, I had learned the difference between toxic shame and healthy shame. (Bradshaw, 1988, 2005) I was no longer the little boy hiding under the bed that felt like a loser. I did not feel less than, unloved, or unwanted anymore. I believed in myself. Believed in my faith. I was embracing Bradshaw's definition of healthy shame. I am a child of God. I am a fallible human being. I am not perfect. I will make mistakes. When that occurs, I am responsible for it. I am responsible for correcting it the best that I can. For making amends. For learning from it and improving my life. I no longer felt like I had to measure up to my dad. In truth, I had heard the story the Cherokee grandfather had told the grandson. There is a war going on within me daily between two spirits; the right wolf and the wicked wolf.[34] The one I will choose to feed is the one that will ultimately win.

---

[34] "A Tale of Two Wolves," author unknown

CHAPTER FIFTEEN:

A New Life Begins

I went back to work for a short while at the auto garage. I was confident. I wanted this new opportunity to turn my life around and have a successful life. My boss convinced me to use my G.I. bill and go to college. He assured me I could still work part-time for him as long as I wanted. I enrolled in a local community college that next term. I had no idea what to take for schooling. My A.A. sponsor suggested Human Services. He was going to college in a similar program. He felt like my experiences could help others with getting their lives back on track. I'd been climaxing on highs and lows for about the last five years. The tops were full of accomplishments, but the lows were low. Each time of hitting bottom meant starting over again. I felt like I had wasted so much time. I was ready to make up for lost time.

I thrived in school and the learning environment! I could not get enough of it. I interviewed for a position in an adolescent residential program as a youth service worker and was hired! My cousin had also set me up on a date with her best friend. Our first date was a roller skating rink! She had a son from a prior marriage that was three years old. He loved to skate. She grew up hanging out at the skating rink in Cedar Rapids. It was the most fun I had had in a long time! We were two people searching for some healing in our lives. I don't believe in coincidences. I had been at my cousin's house several times over the years since we were all in high school. I had never met her friend. I had a 2-3-hour block of time between classes at college, so I decided on a whim to drive over to her house. Her best friend was there. We didn't even speak to each other that day. I came in as she was leaving. She greeted me as she was stepping out the door. I asked my cousin who she was. She told me she was recently single again.

I asked my cousin if she thought her friend would go out on a date with me. She was hesitant. She said she was sure that her friend wasn't ready for a serious relationship yet. I told my cousin that was okay because I didn't even know how to have a serious healthy relationship yet. We could call it friendship dating. So, we did. Our early dating experiences were skating, going to kid's movies; going bowling, and going to stock-car races on Friday nights. All the things her son could enjoy and do with us, too. It reminded me of the platonic relationships before that had some of the most positive feelings of care, compassion, and intimacy. As we got more serious about real dating, my cousin started double dating with us. We both were healthy, happy, and felt like we had a new beginning!

We committed to a dating relationship and engagement. We got married in the Fall. My dad was the best man. It seemed fitting given everything we had been through together. We almost had no rings to exchange. Our house was burglarized a few days before the wedding. The rings, among other things, were stolen. We couldn't afford to replace them. My dad volunteered to come down and take us out to pick out rings and offered to pay for them. I initially declined. Probably my pride. He conveyed that he wanted to do this for us, so I agreed, and we went ring shopping at Wal-Mart. That was my concession; no expensive wedding rings. He came down, and we went shopping. I did appreciate his kindness and generosity. I knew it made him feel good to help us.

The wedding was small, only family and close friends. The minister had known her since she was a child. He and her Grandma were old and dear friends. It was one of the happiest days of my life! It was funny driving home with "Just Married" on the car, with our son sitting on his Mom's lap looking out the window and waving to people passing by in their cars! The looks we were getting were interesting, to say the least! One of those early mornings to follow, I was awakened with a thump on my chest and a little minion smiling down at me saying, "What are we going to do today, Dad?" Now that was priceless!

Another son joined our family the following year. When he was born, I had to call my dad first and let him know we had a boy! It wasn't long, and I was immersed in cub scouts, youth sports, and having fun in my new role as a

Dad. I graduated from the community college with my Associates Degree in Human Services. I had also taken promotions and applied for various positions in juvenile residential treatment settings. Over the next three years, I worked as a youth counselor in residential facilities, boy's homes, a detention center, and a diagnostic & evaluation unit.

I had not embraced coming back to church worship, but I was connected to an active 12 Step community. One of my sponsors named "Tex" was a wise ole' fella. We would visit over coffee at the Industrial Club, and whenever I would go off on a tangent about something, he would calmly listen for a while. Then, he would gently interject the following, "Randy. In a little while, you are going to get up, climb those stairs, and drive away from here. Understand this; it is no longer about him, or her, or whoever you are upset with anymore. You are responsible for your actions. Whether you stay sober or not. Whether you end up in a fight, or whether you end up in jail, you are responsible." Maybe he read Bradshaw's book, too. Thanks, Tex.

In 1984, I applied for a position as a correctional officer in an adult residential correctional facility. I was offered a part-time job that I had to decline. I could not take care of my family unless it were a full-time job. I was already working full time in a boy's home and occasionally picked up overtime shifts. My wife had recently been laid off due to her job liquidating. She had been a convenience store manager and was looking for anything at the time.

The residential supervisor understood, and she called me in for another interview a few months later. I was hired! I was excited and relieved. The wages and benefits were significantly higher in adult corrections than they were in juvenile services. With a family to care for, I needed the promotion and full-time benefits. After about a year working as a correctional officer, though, I knew that if I wanted to try and get promoted, I needed to go back to college to earn my bachelor's degree. For the next two years, I was busy working and going to school full time. I worked at two different facilities to gain experience with probation referrals, parole clients, and a state work-release program for inmates being released back into the community.

In the spring of 1987, I graduated with my Bachelor's Degree in Criminal Justice. I was the first in our family to graduate from post-secondary schooling. I was also promoted to a Probation Officer position in the Judicial District that weekend. To top it off, my wife told me to pick her up a scratch-off lottery ticket when we stopped for gas on the way home. The ticket was a winner;

$10,000. I couldn't believe it! My new boss in the probation unit told me I would probably never have a weekend like that again! The problems and pain of the past were fading away. It seemed like a curse had been lifted, and I was back in God's graces. I would spend the next thirty years working in a fabulous career in Correctional Services.

I loved the work! I thrived on the challenges! I was learning that some of my personal experiences related to those of our clients; either in the facilities or on the community supervision caseloads. I was learning that balanced with appropriate case management skills and counseling techniques; the self-disclosure could selectively have a positive impact. I was receiving excellent feedback from my colleagues that had more experience. I was blessed with exceptional supervisors that mentored me and taught me the responsibilities of the job.

My faith journey had changed, too. When I had enrolled back in school, I transferred to a position at the state work release facility. One of the inmates was a man that had served in the Marines. He saw combat in Vietnam. He was a small built man. He had been a tunnel rat in the war. The Viet Cong were known for building underground tunnel systems. Soldiers of small stature drew the short straw and had to go underground to investigate. He was suffering from residual consequences of the war.

When he arrived at the facility, he was serving the remainder of a 25- year charge for terrorism. He was drunk and had barricaded himself inside his home. He had his young daughter with him. He and his wife had divorced, and she had custody of the kids. He held police at bay with a pellet gun. The Judge sentenced him directly to prison. He had gotten sober in jail. He had also returned to his faith in God. He indeed had changed. He was well liked by all of the staff. When he discharged his sentence, he requested to become a volunteer to try and help other inmates with re-entry issues and assist staff with whatever he was allowed to do. The Residential Manager permitted him to complete a volunteer assistance program with the Volunteer Services Coordinator. He became the first official volunteer at the state work release facility. For me, more than that, he shared his faith. He witnessed to me. Him the inmate and me the keeper of the keys.

After he had discharged his sentence, my boss saw no issues with me mentoring him outside of work. He had joined a local Marine Corps League organization which was essential for his recovery. Being around other veterans, especially combat vets, provided much healing for him. It helped him get past the toxic shame of his terrorism incident. Being active in the league and working with the other members on community service projects helped him feel whole again; an average person and no longer an inmate. He invited my dad and me also to join the league and become a part of their activities. The three of us had a lot in common. We'd all experienced the Cherokee parable of the two wolves. We knew the battle with the flesh and the spirit. And, we had found recovery. The Marine motto, *Semper Fidelis* is Latin for "always faithful". We were also all Marines.

Eventually, he became a close friend to my family and me. My young sons called him, "Uncle Bob." They especially enjoyed mud-running in his Chevy Blazer. I appreciated his commitment to his faith. He was often in prayer; often in the Word. Whenever I would share a problem or issue going on with me, his first response was that we needed to pray, open a bible, and then discuss it. I don't know if he ever shared any of this with the residential manager or not. He was still a volunteer at the work release facility. He was like family to more staff than just me. Whether coincidence or not, it was about this time that my boss invited my wife and me to join them at their church in Marion.

We agreed and visited on a Sunday morning. The Pastor happened to be preaching a sermon about his former days as a bricklayer, and the blue collar world of heavy drinking and abuse that he had also lived before accepting a relationship with Christ. At the end of the service, he greeted people at the door. He smiled, said hello, and then oddly said, "Randy, God has already forgiven you for all of those sins of the past. He only wants to have a relationship with you now." How did he know? What did he know? Neither he nor my boss would ever confirm that they had spoken. It didn't matter. It was the right timing and the right fit. I felt comfortable with this pastor. And, the assistant pastor was also involved in a program he developed for domestic violence perpetrators that became a foundation for batterer's education classes. He would later develop a specialization in grief counseling and hospital chaplaincy. He became an instrumental mentor for me when I became a volunteer as a hospital chaplain.

Dad and I were finally at a pretty good place in our relationship, too. He had agreed to be the best man at my wedding (1981). He had been working hard to make amends to my mom and all of us siblings. He was a wonderful husband, father, and grandfather. Family gatherings were happy times. Filled with a lot of fun, laughs, and good fellowship with each other. We all knew that he sincerely regretted the pain he had caused in the past and that he enjoyed his family being all together. He had been given a gift always to be grateful for and never take for granted.

He was happy to see me come into a career of my own so removed from anything he would ever do. He had encouraged me not to try and be like him anymore. He was proud of me; of who I had become. Glad that I enjoyed the work that I was doing. It seemed odd, but I was beginning to enjoy working on projects with him. Repairing a car, roofing a house, fixing an appliance, doing some home repairs. It was fun. I was learning a lot from him. He had changed. I had changed. Our relationship was different. It showed how well we could work together on things now. I had a young family of my own with a home in need of improvements and repairs. I was never an excellent handyman. That was one of my dad's better skills. So, he often came down to visit and to help out. We were finally getting along pretty well.

By the late 1980's I was living and raising my family in a small town east of Cedar Rapids. It was a fresh start for my wife and I both. She had also grown up in a chaotic, dysfunctional family riddled with abuse. She loved her family, but also wanted some distance and boundaries. Within about an hour we could visit her family or mine. The Methodist minister that had married us had previously served the congregation of the small town we now lived in and made our home. He still knew many of the families there. He introduced us to some beautiful older couples that were like grandparents to us and our sons. And, we met other couples our age that was raising their children, too.

It was hard to leave the friends we had made at the Marion Methodist church, but we were only moving some 15 miles away. We had found our home in Springville. I would stay connected with some of the men from the Marion church through United Methodist Men activities and the Walk to Emmaus spiritual retreats that I had become involved with as mission work. I volunteered to serve on walks as a table leader, support staff, and kitchen helper.

We were all healing; at least solidly on that path. My older sister had met a wonderful man that accepted her son as his own. They would go on to have another son, too. My next younger sister and her husband were back from his Army tour and lived in the Northeast Iowa area. He began a career in law enforcement which he still continues to serve in today. They would have a son that would also join their family. And, my younger sister was married with a son, daughter, and step-daughter. We all had strong connections to our faith and attended local churches where we had found love & support. Eventually, all of the "Brewer Street Kids" would work in a professional human services field. We all felt compelled to help others. Inspiring hope in the darkest of times has become so important to us as siblings. And, eventually, we all became grandparents!

My older sister worked in a nursing home facility specializing in service to the patients dealing with dementia and Alzheimer's disease. My next younger sister would also work in residential care facilities for adults specializing in recreational and occupational activities. And, my youngest sister would work in a senior community center specializing in meeting the daily living needs of the elderly. We all had helpful people along the way that chose to mentor us; befriend us; hear each of our stories of survival, and gave us an opportunity to give back; to pay it forward. It all started out when we were toddlers climbing into a seat on a Sunday School bus; very broken and wounded kids. A handful of people in that Baptist Church decided only to love us; to love our folks; to offer us hope and the faith to believe that life could be different. And, now it finally was.

CHAPTER SIXTEEN:

The Call

In 1990, I was working as an intensive supervision parole officer. I had a caseload of clients that were violent offenders and drug offenders. I had gotten used to the pace of managing both a workload and college studies, so after I had graduated it felt like I had quite a bit of time on my hands. I didn't have as much time as I thought because I was also volunteering in my sons' youth activities. I served as a cub scout leader, youth group leader, Sunday School teacher, and little league coach. Fortunately, my wife was the wizard behind the curtain that worked to keep all of the obligations of those volunteer roles organized. Most of what I had to do was simply show up and facilitate a meeting, be an emcee, lead a prepared lesson, or coach ball games with kids that were in the capable hands of great assistant coaches, anyway.

I applied for a part-time job as a group facilitator in a local intra-familial sexual abuse treatment program. I co-facilitated an educational, social skills group with children that had been sexually abused by a family member. Sexual abuse treatment was a new area of learning for me. I was working with specialized clinicians. It was only a two-hour group one night a week. The director of the program was a recognized and respected specialist in this field. She put new facilitators through an on-the-job training program with experienced facilitators. I was still working full time as a parole officer for the Judicial District.

The director had also asked me to facilitate an educational treatment group with the sexual offenders. I politely declined, explaining that I worked full time with other kinds of violent criminals and had no desire to work with sex offenders. My older sister had not yet shared her secret with anyone other than the College, campus minister. She had taken the minister's advice to confront our dad, though. He not only told her to face him, but to say explicitly to him that she had told the minister at college. The minister had learned enough to know that there was power in the secret and that the first step to getting the abuse to stop is to tell. The second phase is to let the perpetrator know it is no longer a secret.

At some point, she also confronted our mom with the truth. Mom initially didn't want to believe it. She thought she was lying. Then, she blamed her daughter for somehow causing it to happen. She denied ever knowing that it had happened, but that wouldn't match later accounts. Dad admitted to the abuse to his wife, initially telling her that it had only happened one time. He would later take full responsibility. Mom's response was to tell my older sister that there was nothing that would change it now. What's done is done. We just needed to move on and get it behind us. She was adamant that no one else was told, not even us siblings. Mom was convinced that nothing good would ever come from telling the rest of us. At the time, my dad was not ready for that can of worms being opened, either. He was more than happy to let sleeping dogs lie, hopefully, never to awaken.

I would go on to renege on my former position of not having any desire to work with sex offenders. Two sisters that were in the intra-familial program were finally making some pleasing steps toward learning to trust again. One night, the youngest girl mustered up the courage to ask me for an appropriate over the shoulder hug! I was happily amazed! She had not even spoken in weeks. She struggled to smile or make eye contact. Her perpetrator was her step-dad. I was a big guy at the time; about 250 lbs. Her stepping out in faith to trust me had not gone unnoticed. The director had also seen it. After the girls and their family had gone, she approached me while I was filling out some group notes. She told me matter-of-factly that if real professionals were not willing to work with the perpetrators there would continue to be more victims. She asked me to reconsider my position on not working with sex offenders.

The Judicial District Department of Correctional Services (DCS) had started a sex offender program at the probation office in about 1987. I went and talked to the sex offender program supervisor and the program manager, Jack. I wanted to get some more information about transferring into the unit. There were not any transfers open at that time, but they were expecting a probation officer to be transferring out soon. Since I had about one year of experience working in the intra-familial sexual abuse program at the other agency, the program manager invited me to sit in and observe the group process in the correctional services program and shadow him. His only requirement was first to tell me the following, "Randy before you decide you want to work in the sex offender unit, think about seeing some horrible crime scene photos and reading about some of the most awful crimes imaginable. I mean so disgusting that you want to go outside and punch the wall or puke. And, when you come back into this office and sit in this chair, you can look across this desk and still see another human being staring back at you. You need to see a person that can change. If you are not able to do that, then do not request a transfer to my unit."

I thought about what Jack had said. I thought about what the director of the other intra-familial program had said. I believed that I could still see someone as a human being despite their sexual offending. I felt I could work with them to make those positive changes, so there were not more victims, like the little girl that had such a significant impact on me. I sat in on groups; I shadowed with Jack, and in a short while, a full-time probation officer position opened up within the unit.

The Iowa Board for the Treatment of Sexual Abusers (IBTSA) had also recently formed and had a professional certification program in place for sex offender treatment providers (SOTP). The probation officers that worked in the sex offender programs were also required to become certified and co-facilitate treatment groups. For the next year, my time was spent on learning everything I could about sexual offenders, sexual abuse, and sex offender treatment. I earned my first certification in 1993. That training and certification helped prepare me for handling the phone call I was about to receive.

I was sitting at home on a Saturday morning. Saturdays were house cleaning days. When the phone rang, I assumed it was probably something to do with work. It was the norm on weekends to get calls at home from a jail interviewer or pre-trial release counselor about a current or former client who was arrested and facing pending charges. Clients would also frequently call for travel permission or to report changes in work schedules. It was my mom, though. And by the sound of her voice, I knew she was upset. My mind was racing about what it could be. Who was hurt? What had happened? She told me that she was worried about my dad. He had not been himself lately. She said that he was having a difficult time forgiving himself over something from the past. At that point, it wasn't as surprising for the call. Working a 12 Step recovery program was part of both our lives for many years. We were both sober. We were part of each other's support system. But, when she said that Dad was saying things like he would be better off dead, things beyond forgiveness, and she was worried about him hurting or killing himself, that was over the top! I had never thought of my dad as being someone that would consider suicide, let alone ever attempt it. My mom had her issues with neurotic behavior, and I figured she was overreacting. She asked me if I would drive up to their home, pick him up, go for a hike outdoors, and see if he would talk to me. I told her, "Sure," and was about to tell her goodbye and get ready for the drive. It was going to take me a little over an hour to get there. I didn't understand all the drama, but the only way to know what was going on with him, and her for that matter, was to pay them a visit. Before I could tell her goodbye, though, she told me not to hang up. She said, "Randy, your older sister has something to say to you before you come up to see your dad. I'll put her on the phone."

My older sister, Rhonda, took the phone and gave a nervous laugh. Rhonda's throat cleared, and she said that there was something about Dad that she had wanted to tell me for a long time, but she just didn't know how. At that moment, things became crystal clear. The last family puzzle piece fell into place. She said my name, and then I finished the statement for her. I said, "I already know what you are about to tell me. Dad sexually abused you when we were kids." I don't remember everything she said, but I do remember that she cried. She apologized to me for not telling me sooner. She explained that she wanted to say something when I first came home from the military but was afraid of me doing something I would regret. She said she tried to disclose what happened in the only way she could when we were kids; by telling us that none of us knew what was going on.

I tried to reassure her that everything was going to be okay and that I would talk to her when I got there. I hung up the phone, but my mind was racing. People talk about their lives flashing before them when they are about to die. Our childhood flashed before me when I hung up that phone. I had flashbacks of childhood memories that would soon be confirmed by my sister, Dad, and my mom as real and not imagined. I guess the pain and trauma of the incidents were enough to force me to push the memories to the darkest, deepest, depths of my mind. Now, they just came flooding in.

I already had the painful memories of the driving lessons. Now I realized why she pleaded with me to get in the car and ride along. It was to stop the abuse. I remembered all of the times I would drag my pillow and blanket to the living room and sprawl out in front of the Warm Morning stove blower. Now, I knew why Dad tried to sneak into us kids' bedroom.

Some of the memories previously blocked were of waking up at night to hear my older sister crying on the bottom bunk bed with my dad sitting on the edge of her bed. A memory of waking up to hear my mom scream my father's name and then ask him "what the hell he was doing?" Mom was standing in the bedroom doorway. He was sitting on the edge of my sister's bunk bed. Numerous memories of my mom going to bed after taking prescription tranquilizers and needing to rest. She put my older sister in charge to babysit us. When Dad would come home from the tavern drunk he would be "out of it"; staggering around, stumbling. He would undo the zipper of his trousers and expose himself to my older sister as she just tried to get him into bed with Mom. As kids, we just thought he was drunk; confused; trying to find the bathroom. I remembered waking up to intense arguments occurring late at night. Sometimes, just my mom and Dad. At other times, both of them and my older sister. One of these was after she (sister) had dropped out of college. I remember my dad blaming the campus minister and accusing him of illicit acts with her. Blaming her for being so rebellious when she left home. Not being smarter about protecting herself. Mom was buying into his story and confronting my sister along this path, too. I remember my older sister telling her things like if she only knew the truth. My dad was angry and shouted that was enough, and the discussion was over. He got up and was slamming things down; slamming things around; pacing back and forth.

I would often stare out my bedroom window into the night when these incidents would occur and dissociate until I could fall back asleep. Now it was evident. I could not see it then. Or, my mind would not allow me to face it. It all made sense now. At least it was starting to make more sense. I had about an hour and a half to drive to try to figure out what to say to my dad; to decide what to do. And, to determine how to finally be there for my sister. I was feeling guilty. I was feeling ashamed. I was angry, confused, and unsure of myself. I was her only brother. Her brother that was directed by the Colonel to protect her;

protect all of his sisters. The Colonel had made me promise when I was sitting on his lap in that blue overstuffed chair when I was seven. I had failed. Now, what was I going to do to make up for that somehow?

When I got to my parent's house, my dad was outside doing something. Dad being outside gave me a chance to give my mom and older sister a hug and tell them that I loved them. Everything would be okay. I went to find Dad. I gave him a manly hug like had become a customary greeting for us. As I recall, it was Late-Summer or early Fall, and the ginseng digging season had just begun. He enjoyed traipsing through the woods digging root. We had been doing it together since I was maybe 12 years old. I suggested that we go to Turtle Creek Park and hit the trails, walk the woods, and see if we could spot any ginseng. He said okay and got his old fedora, walking stick, and digging hoe. We took his old green Ford truck which had lots of memories full of coon hunts, too. When we parked and got out of the truck, I came around to his driver's side and stopped him as he was exiting. I only said, "I know what you did to Rhonda."

I did grab him by the shoulders, although he offered no resistance. I made some reference to feeling like kicking his ass unless he could give me a reason to listen to him. He cried, visibly shaken; broken. He said, "I wish you would. Just do something to take me out of this life. I can never make things right. What I did to her was unforgivable."

He went on to do an A.A. 12 Step- Fifth Step; "We admitted to God, to ourselves, and to another human being the exact nature of our wrongs."[35] I assume that he had already done this step with Bill or one of his other sponsors. However, I'm confident that he had not disclosed his sexual sins. He knew that I had recently transferred to the sex offender unit and was learning the many new aspects of this field. He had often complimented me on choosing to work in human services and help the kids in the group homes, as well as the adults in the corrections centers. He understood that many of them also had histories of alcohol abuse, violence, and had made poor choices that they regretted. He thought that God had played the major role in guiding me into this field. Maybe the transfer into the sex offender unit finally was the catalyst that brought him to a place of facing his last hidden demon? My sister

---

[35] The Big Book of Alcoholics Anonymous

had already confronted him years earlier. However, there wasn't closure; only moving on, and not talking about it again.

As he spoke, he took pretty good responsibility for the abuse. Especially given no involvement in any formal treatment. He was able to convey that his abuse of Rhonda probably contributed to her problems in college, and some failed relationships with older men. He felt guilty over her having her first son out of wedlock and being a single Mom. He admitted that that was why he had become so close to his grandson, and tried to help them all he could. He was glad that she had met a kind man that loved her, loved her son, and had married her. Dad admitted that day in the woods that he could never undo the harm or make up for the pain caused her. My father promised to make amends the best he could for the rest of his life.

Although he still owned the house we grew up in, he had moved a few years before to another house in town. It was close to the home place; just two streets west and along the river. Eventually, when his renter moved out, he sold the house to her on contract with small monthly payments. Rhonda and her family were needing a place to live. It was one of the ways that he could take some action to try and repair some of the harm. He was worried that the rest of us might be upset about her getting the home place. None of us were. We told him as far as we were concerned, he could just give it to her. That was between them to work out.

He also talked about the hell he had put my mom through. Not just the sexual abuse of her daughter, but the affair, his womanizing, his drinking. He commented, "You know, Rand,' she should have never stayed. She had a thousand reasons through the years to leave me. I don't deserve her. If she had done the same to me, I know I would never have stayed. I put her through hell. And, she had already been through hell with her own Dad and brother. I can't make it up to her. I can't ever make it right. But, I will die trying. Our friends always tease your mother that all she has to do is tell me that she wants something, and I'll get it for her. If they only knew the truth, they would maybe understand. I can never do enough for her to make up for what I have done that's hurt her."

He had changed and was making amends. He took trips wherever Mom wanted to go. After working all day, he came home to start dinner. After dinner, Dad cleared the table and did the dishes while she rested. He would take her out after dinner for ice cream, or for coffee and a visit to someone's home for a while. Just because she wanted to get out, go for a ride, and see some people for a while.

Mom had severe mental health issues and emotional instability. Beautiful lady; very loving; very caring. But, she was a constant worrier. Sadly, the neurosis mom suffered only got worse over time as she got older, compared to when she was younger. She had experienced a couple of nervous breakdowns when we were kids. She was on some heavy tranquilizers and sedatives. Often back then, as the old expression goes, "she didn't know whether she was on foot or horseback." She was often out of it. It was totally understandable as an adult. The mind will do what it has to survive; even shut down. It was confusing as a child. There wasn't any way to understand it.

It wasn't always like that. There were periods of time that she worked out of the home a few hours a day cleaning houses for people for extra money. And, she tended garden and strawberry beds with all of our help. And, when she was well and healthy, she was an awesome cook and baker! We would come home from school to a table lined up with homemade pies, cakes, cookies, and fabulous meals. That was on her good days. Looking back, it's not hard to see that the breakdowns coincided with the heights of heavy drinking, abuse, and turmoil. She simply couldn't deal with it. Or, could she? The vicious cycle at work here was that when Mom fell apart, Dad would have to get it together. He would be "on the wagon" again; sober for a while. Dad was coming home from work to get supper ready for us kids and Mom. He helped us with our homework. We would often play family board games, or pop popcorn on the stove and watch TV together. Abuse cycles are complicated.

I need to get back to the woods and our talk. Dad admitted that Mom had some serious emotional problems. He acknowledged that although her father had been violent towards her and contributed to some of her problems, he was to blame for most of it.

After Dad died and Mom lived alone, there were three of us that still lived in town. I had just moved back home about six months before my dad died. I was divorced, and starting over again as a single man. My oldest son enlisted in the Navy, and my youngest was in high school living with his Mom, although we had joint custody. So, after Dad died, I spent a lot of time checking in on Mom. I stopped about every night after work. On Sundays, after church, I would take Mom out for lunch or dinner. Two of my sisters had always lived in our hometown, and the other sister lived in a town about 40 minutes west; not too far away. We were all close.

Mom was prone to calling one of us (actually, all of us until someone answered!) and she would be in a panic. She was worried over something or needed something picked up at the store. It was always an emergency. Nothing could wait! There were many times that my sisters were exhausted from all the running and would say, "I don't know how Dad did it!" "I don't know how he ever put up with her!" We were all convinced that he had made a pact with God that this was part of his penance for all of the years of hell he had put her through. He did it with a smile and without complaint most of the time. He would do whatever he needed to do to calm her fears and get her to relax.

He got her out socializing with others that she enjoyed being with to have some fun. These were usually brief visits. They may drive anywhere from 10 minutes to an hour to visit a friend or family member. No sooner than the coffee poured, Mom was getting anxious, nervous, and telling Dad it was about time to be going home. He and whoever were the guests would reassure her that everything was okay, and there was plenty of time to get home and get things done before bed. God blessed my mom with some beautiful, amazing, friends!

With Dad gone, my sisters would often call me in their frustrations and ask me to stop in more, visit more, and get Mom out more. They reasoned that out of the four of us kids; I had probably contributed the most to her neurosis during my years as the wayward prodigal son. It was only fair that I show up and help out more. I agreed with them. Between the Colonel, her brother, our dad, and then me, I did not know how she had any sanity left at all. And, I would conclude that spending more time with her was the least that I could do. Crazy as it sounds, I enjoyed it and seldom was stressed over her anxiety attacks and obsessing fears. The time spent was good therapy for the both of us.

I don't recall very much about what else took place that day in the woods. When we came back into town, I visited with Mom & Dad both for a while. We prayed. I reassured them things would be okay; that we would get through this one day at a time. I checked in with my older sister. I listened as she talked. She was worried about Dad. She said that although she hated what had happened to her, she had already forgiven him. She was relieved that our younger sisters evaded sexual abuse. With her secret finally disclosed, we all finally started the healing journey together. We were all at different stages of the voyage, and quite frankly, we still are.

Rhonda was finally able to begin to tell us how things were different for her than the rest of us. She was able to verbalize why she was so angry at Dad and Mom. Rhonda was able to express why never telling anyone seemed like the only choice. She had a voice, again. She was taking back the power taken from her. Some scars and wounds last a long time, though. These are what therapists call trauma bonds. Even today, as we get into some petty sibling squabble, Rhonda can become very upset at our failing to understand her circumstances. She has a tendency to lash verbally out like that wounded girl that survived the unimaginable, without any of us knowing or understanding what she was going through. After lashing out, Rhonda feels awful. She is consumed with regret until she makes amends with us. Knowing that it is the little girl inside herself reacting on an emotional level doesn't change wanting to fight for some sense of being heard. She knows we all love her, and would go to any length to help her. Yes, surviving incest abuse is complicated; for both the direct victims and the indirect victims within the family.

After our mom had died five years ago (2011), we began to describe ourselves as adult orphans. We knew that all we had was each other. We made a pact to get together for sibling retreats at least every Spring and Fall. We take turns in planning the events and hosting. These have become delightful expressions of healing. We have fun in each other's company. We look forward to every retreat. The bond between us just gets stronger. We understand each other's pain more. We understand each other's perspectives more. Some of the time, we are engaged in thoughtful reflection. We try to help each other make sense out of something that has remained a stumbling block for one of us. We've learned not to judge. We mainly listen and offer insights. We cry. We tease each other. We laugh together. We joke with each other. We listen to each of us talk about our lives. We talk about things important to us. We live for the moment of being in each other's company, not knowing when one of us will be gone. We love our time together and cherish our sibling retreats. We pray for each other, and with each other. We forgive each other when one of us has the courage to bring up a painful memory of the past, still unresolved. We heal, together.

CHAPTER SEVENTEEN:

Epilogue

My dad died in September of 2000. He had a 25- year sobriety anniversary coin that he carried in his pocket. He had a recognizable faith in God for about 20 of those years. He was not a religious man. He had become a spiritual person. He found solace and closeness with God more often on a trout stream, hiking the woods, sitting around a campfire, reading his Bible in his recliner at night, or in preparation for Christmas and knowing the holiday would bring all of us together for food and fellowship. Without question, the last ten years of his life as a new creation in Christ was his happiest and most rewarding. Although he loved country music, it was the country gospel that he mostly listened to in the last years of his life. He enjoyed sending money to faith-based youth-related charities and enjoyed reading the newsletters that were sent with a thank you card in return. He looked forward to visiting all four of us kids and spending a day with each of us to catch up with our families. Although not big on regular church attendance, he frequently talked Mom into coming to a Sunday service with our family as they made road trips to visit us. He had become one of the kindest, compassionate, patient, and most understanding men I have ever known. It was hard not to like him. It was not hard to love him. The bond he had with each family member grew stronger over time. Forgiveness had taken root, and the pain and abuse of the past did fade into memories as they were overshadowed by the person he became.

Apparently, trauma bonds still existed. Residual consequences of that level of abuse and violence have lingering effects in most people's lives. We were all healing, though. And, we continue to heal today. It's been sixteen years since his death. I would give almost anything to be able to trout fish with him again. To listen to him sing those old country gospel songs. To drink coffee at the table, sit on the porch, work on a car, or build a project with him. Share a meal with him. Open the Bible and pray with him.

His other children and grandchildren would list all of the things they wish they could still do with him if he were here. Like the Native American grandfather in the parable, he had learned that it was his choice which wolf he fed, and that choice would determine which wolf would exist. He chose to feed the real wolf, the decent, respectable one, and the fruits of the Spirit were plentiful. He made a concerted effort to keep the evil wolf at bay. He was not perfect, but he was ready and alert to when his ego, pride, or anger was surfacing. He was quick to apologize when he sensed that he had upset or offended someone. He wanted to resolve things peaceful. He did not like to fight. He did not like to quarrel. He did not like conflict. He was no longer aggressive. He wasn't passive; not a doormat, either. He had learned to become assertive. He had learned to serve God and not himself.

While he had liked being the center of attention as his former self, he now loved helping others, and more quietly existing in the background. While he had once thrived on power and control, he now embraced egalitarian relationships with others, especially family. Yes, he was right. I could hate him for my childhood. Some of it was a living hell. However, I also had to thank him for some parts of my childhood. He insisted we board the bus every Sunday and go to Sunday School. The ties and relationships formed at that little church would set this journey of healing into motion. And, I certainly have to thank him for my adulthood. At least a part of the person I have become. My work ethic, desire to serve others, and my choice to feed the right wolf are all reflections of him. My commitment to serve God and others comes back to his example.

Another illustration of the kindness he bestowed, is how he cared for feral cats in his neighborhood. When we were young kids, he was not a cat fan. Honestly, he had no time for cats. I don't think he valued them at all. He liked dogs for family pets, as well as for work purposes; hunting dogs. We convinced him to let us bring a kitten from the farm home once. His mom loved cats. So we used that against him. One night after dinner, the kitten had gotten up on the table to eat some scraps; just being a typical kitten that needed to learn. He became furious and tossed the kitten down into the basement. He wanted to do away with the cat. We begged him to keep it. The kitten would not have another chance if it got up on the table around food again. He was not joking. He was dead serious.

Now, as an older, kind man, he had a gentle spirit. He assisted his neighbor, Judy, with caring for the feral cats in the neighborhood. He put out food and water for them, as well as bowls of milk. He talked to them. He coaxed them to come in close so he could pet them. He named most of them. These were feral cats that most of us could not get close to, let alone touch! He had become some cat whisperer. The cats liked him. They sensed that he cared about them; their needs, and that he was safe to be around. He came to enjoy them so much as he was out in the yard gardening, and they would wander up for a visit.

Many of them were suffering from genetic disabilities from in-breeding; physical disabilities that were apparent. They walked funny. They stumbled and swayed back and forth. They did not seem to be tracking well mentally, either. Just like the scriptures praise all creatures great and small as being important to the Creator, these feral cats were important to my dad. Maybe it was another penance? Perhaps, a part of his healing? He made their lives better than they would have been without him.

Because of their disabilities, many of them did not have very long lifespans. He had his favorites. When he discovered that one had passed away, he grieved. He mourned. He missed a friend. Maybe he could empathize with their disabilities, too? Although he had recovered from his crippling disease, he still walked with a noticeable limp. Sometimes, it was more apparent than others. When working in the garden or around the flower beds, there were times he simply had to get off his feet and rest. He often used a walking stick as a cane. Maybe his experience was like the Apostle Paul's "thorn in the flesh"[36] That might have been a physical infirmity that God chose not to remove. He also decided not to remove my dad's crippling disease entirely. Maybe God used it to promote empathy, compassion, kindness, and love for feral cats; a creature he once viewed as lesser and not even worthy of life.

---

[36] II Corinthians, Chapter 12: 7-10; Paul talks about his affliction that God did not totally remove.

CHAPTER EIGHTEEN:

Reflections

I want to leave readers with a few takeaway thoughts for those who have stayed with me page after page on this journey. For those of you who are also survivors of sexual abuse and violence within your families, there is hope! There is a help; more so today, than when we were kids. There are professional treatment providers and victim services specialists that are available to assist you on a journey toward healing. For the indirect victims of familial abuse, I hope that this sharing of our journey will provide some of the answers to questions that you have had, and provide some insight for how to move forward and heal.

For the professionals that were willing to read this book, it is important that I clarify a few things. While I hope that my reliving of our experience with familial abuse does help you with your work, it wasn't written as a workbook or guide. I believe it could be a supplement to some treatment curricula. Possibly a group assignment could come from it, or an individual project for a client struggling with similar issues. Most of the story is going back to describe the life of a young boy, and looking at life through his eyes. I was trying to explain the impact of familial abuse through his lenses. I know some clients and families can read this, relate to it, and begin a healing journey of their own. With the transparency of the issues and the complex dynamics involved, maybe there would be value to discussing it at your staff meetings or unit gatherings. If this book can provide some hope, healing, or good for any of those purposes, praise God. I wrote the book for those reasons.

In my opinion, the most important takeaway is that this book can open communication between the primary disciplines represented in sex offender management, specifically the treatment providers and enforcement officials. For sex offender treatment to work effectively, it requires a collaborative, supportive, partnership to exist within these disciplines. "One size fits all" approaches are not comprehensive.[37] We know that. Google it. There are volumes of research out there now confirming this truth for each of the disciplines. Treatment providers that want to produce the best results from their programs need to incorporate evidence-based, risk-need-response (RNR) principles, in a risk management driven program. (CSOM National Resource Group, 2008) No one can say anything with certainty for each client. However, that's true in the world of actuaries in business, health care, and insurance, also. The best we can do is learn to identify profiles, based upon valid risk assessment, and provide the treatment dosage and level of intensity recommended for that profile.

Effective treatment strategies with sexual abusers, in some ways, mirror what we know about adult learning theories. Adults need to know there is a purpose to the learning. Building positive relationships is a fundamental component to successful learning. Learning in a group facilitated format tends to yield positive outcomes. Allowing clients to take responsibility and ownership for their learning produces better results. Focusing on their strengths, rather than their deficits, is more fruitful. Applying the right strategy to the right client will optimize learning and growth. (Knowles, Holton, & A., 2012)

The same applies to the enforcement side. Low-risk offenders, by the whole, do not require the intensity of implementation measures that the high-risk profiles need. Low-risk offenders, in general, are pretty self-correcting when caught and identified. That seems to be true, whether we provide specialized treatment for them or not. Putting low-risk offenders in the elevated treatment track, with intensive supervision standards, produces poor results. We keep doing it. While we over-treat and over-supervise the low-risk group, we under-treat and under-supervise the highest risk group, due to resulting limitations in those resources.

Unanimously, all four of us siblings are relieved that the sexual abuse that occurred within our home did not play out in the current public, political,

---

[37] Note: "Ancient Ethics for Today's Healers", by Geral Blanchard (2014)

legislative, or legal climate concerning sexual abusers. We are convinced that our family or any of us individually would not be better as a result of current approaches. For me, speaking as the sibling with the most knowledge in this area, this is not a polarized issue for us. We collectively agree that the centuries-old approach of "what happens in a family stays in a family" was not appropriate. It was wrong for society, and specifically our legal system, to turn a blind eye to abuse within a family because of a belief that a "man's home was his castle" and his wife and children were little more than property.[38]

We collectively agree that the current approach of criminal prosecution and severe penalties does not yield the best results. Once caught and given some formal intervention, intra-familial incest offenders have the lowest rates of recidivism. However, based upon criminal code statutes, their offenses can carry some of the strictest penalties. For instance, in some jurisdictions, an intra-familial offender would also have a "special sentence" parole of either ten years or a lifetime, that would follow the sentencing sanctions for the original sexual offense. Sex offender registries (SOR) comprise a tier system which has registration requirements based upon crime code statutes, and not validated risk assessments. For example, Tier 1 offenders are required to check in annually, while Tier 3 offenders are required to comply with a quarterly check in as directed. Often, when the offense is against a child, a lifetime sex offender registry (SOR) requirement is mandated.[39] While some sex offender registry websites make the disclaimer that the tier system is an identification system for law enforcement and not a risk assessment, it is a natural assumption for most people to associate stricter reporting requirements and enhanced penalties with the most dangerous of sex offenders. However, this is often not the case.

Historically, the sex offenders responsible for the most heinous sexual crimes have fueled legislation since the national registry laws were enacted in the mid-1990's. Many of the sex offender laws that have swept the country since the mid-2000's have followed that same trend. Most of these dangerous

---

[38] Public records revealed only a handful of child sexual abuse cases in the 1970's. Cases rarely made it to the attention of the authorities ("Sexual Abuse in America: Epidemic of the 21st Century" by Longo, Blanchard, 1998)

[39] This example is of the tier system on the Iowa Sex Offender Registry (SOR). However, states are required to comply with federal law enacting the "Adam Walsh Child Protection and Safety Act of 2006" which established national guidelines.

sex offenders have elevated risk factors increasing the probability of sexual offense recidivism; young; prior sex offense; prior violence conviction; lengthy criminal record; non-contact sex offense conviction; unrelated victim; stranger victim; male victim. (Hanson, R.K.; Harris, A.; Phenix, A.; Thorton, D., 2003)

The problem with these most dangerous high-risk sex offenders being the group that fuels legislation is that they represent a small fraction of sex offenders; approximately 1-18.7 %.[40] With our systems of labels and identification, we have created a sense of homogeneity with sex offenders. When, in reality, sex offenders are a heterogeneous group. For instance, according to a Center for Sex Offender Management report published in 2001, incest offenders had observed sexual recidivism rates ranging from 4-10%. Incest offenders are the lowest of any group, as compared to rapists (7-35%), Child molesters with female victims (10-29%), Child molesters with male victims (13-40%), and exhibitionists (41-71%). (Bynum, T.; Carter, M.; Matson, S.; Onley, C., 2001)

When I began my specialized career, it was in an intra-familial sexual abuse treatment program. That was in the early 1990's. Although some of the referrals came from criminal court sentencing orders, many came from referrals from social workers as a condition of a developing child in need of assistance (CINA) petition, or case permanency plan resulting from a founded child sexual abuse report. The court of minors services, and not the adult criminal court, was requiring the successful completion of specialized treatment. Some of these cases were in a diversionary program which could be used as a motivator for the perpetrator to complete sex offender treatment successfully to avoid adult prosecution. Since the trend has pushed further toward the punishment realm, most diversionary programs no longer exist.

As one county attorney told me, "Randy, who wants to be the county attorney in today's climate concerning sex offenders that choose not to prosecute?" The fear of being viewed by the general public or media as soft on sex offenders has made it difficult for prosecutors, legislators, and judiciary to apply discretionary measures. Often, the sex offense risk profile the person has doesn't impact sentencing and enhanced penalties at all. Crime code statutes usually drive these decisions.

---

[40] Note: Static 99-R estimated percentiles; www.static99.org

Another reality is that even being identified as "Low risk" does not mean "no risk." Some sex offenders identified as low risk, by validated specialized assessment measures, will offend with another sexual crime within their lifetime. The percentage of sexual re-offense for the most moderate risk group of offenders is small. Numerous research studies confirm this. In our Iowa validation study of the Iowa Sex Offender Risk Assessment (ISORA) the lowest risk group of offenders had observed sexual or violent offense recidivism rates ranging from .03- 2.8%. (Prell, 2010). However, when news of a sex offense hits the media, there is a tendency to abandon the research, leave best practices, and apply a one size fits all approach. The emotional response is understandable. However, the increasing punishments placed on all offenders, to eradicate sexual abuse, is not very effective sex offender management. And, it's not working. Rape and child molestation is a social problem; just like drug addiction, alcoholism, gambling compulsions, and domestic violence. Legislation and criminal justice involvement is a part of the solution, but it won't eradicate the problem; not any more than our 30-year war on drugs will. (Glass, 2010).[41] Our best hope is through education, increased awareness, prevention, and treatment.

My older sister wanted the sexual abuse to stop. Although I did not fully comprehend what was happening, something was going on with my older sister, perpetrated by my dad, that I also wanted to stop. As a family, we all wanted the multitude of abuses, and the alcoholism, to stop. My older sister's greatest fear of ever reporting the sexual abuse was her removal from the home, my father's incarceration, and our family never being together again. That was also my greatest fear preventing me from ever reporting the physical abuse.

When I shared this manuscript with my siblings, my younger sisters disclosed that they began to question our family dynamics as teenagers. They were starting to make sense of the fragmented relationships. For both of them, understanding the depth of the familial abuse contributed to their decisions to marry at a young age. That was the survival response readily available for them. As one sibling put it, the more time she was able to spend with her boyfriend's

---

[41] President Reagan is often cited for creating the "War on Drugs" in a 1982 speech. President Nixon first used the expression in 1971 and made it accessible. Many policies date back to the Harrison Narcotics Tax Act of 1914, during President Woodrow Wilson's presidency.

family, the more she was forced to confront the dysfunction of her own. When he enlisted in the Army and proposed, her acceptance came without hesitation. She was learning about love and healthy relationships that were not conditional.

We were all like passengers aboard a sinking ship. We had become alerted to the fact that the ship was capsizing, and we needed to flee. Being good at survival, we seized the life boats most readily available for us; college, the military; marriage. An amazing realization for us, as we have discussed the familial abuse and our collective journey of healing, is how God's divine intervention was present and guiding each of our distinct paths.

Keep in mind that the Child Abuse Prevention & Treatment Act did not come about until 1974.[42] Judith Herman's book, "Father-Daughter Incest" was first published in 1981.[43] It was one of the first books to discuss her clinical study as a psychiatrist with female survivors of incest abuse. It was one of the early books to describe the incestuous family; the dysfunction on multiple levels; the complex relationships within those family systems. (Herman, 1981)

My older sister was graduating from high school and leaving for college in 1974. I was already in high school. At that time, any prevention, education, or family intervention programs were just in their infancy stages. It wasn't until the mid-1980's, with the McMartin daycare case from Los Angeles (1984), that sexual abuse became a focal point of discussion within the public and media.[44] The "Oprah Winfrey Show" aired in the mid-1980's, and she also publicly disclosed her being a survivor of sexual abuse.[45] Oprah has used her position and influence to bring about education, awareness, and healing through numerous talk show discussions with her interviewing survivors. (Harpo Studios Productions, 2005) Marilyn Vandebur, crowned Miss

---

[42] Note: Congress created more sexual abuse laws as a result of the National Abuse Coalition formed in 1979. The Child Abuse Victim's Rights Act followed in 1986.

[43] Herman was a Harvard professor that discovered that many women she interviewed in her medical residency were survivors of incest abuse.

[44] This case was interesting due to the number of children reporting abuse, the interview techniques in question, and how foreign some accounts were. In the end, there were no convictions in the case.

[45] 1986 Oprah Winfrey TV show

America in 1957, also disclosed her ordeal as an incest survivor in about the mid-1980's. (Van Debur Atlar, 1991) Incest abuse was perpetrated upon her by her father for about 13 years.[46]

Her father had died about one year before her disclosing the secret to her mother. My parents are dead now, as are most of their closest friends and family from their generation. I would not have had the courage to write this book had they still been living, nor would I have had my older sister's permission to disclose her ordeal until after their death. It is still with some reluctance that my youngest sisters have given their approval. Their recollection of our home environment and the lenses they look back through are different than mine. By the time they had reached their formative years, things were seldom violent, less abusive, and more stable, except our older sister's secret, she could not yet share with any of us.

Had a diversionary intra-familial sexual abuse treatment program been available in the late 1960's to early 1970's, I do believe that particular type of program would have benefited our family more than most approaches. We know from current research on sexual offense recidivism that reporting the abuse to someone in authority, outside the family, is key to stopping the harm. We also know that some formal intervention is an important role in the reduction of future sexual offending. And, we are aware that successful completion of sex offender treatment significantly reduces recidivism. According to the research, incest offenders have the lowest rates of sexual recidivism. (Bynum, T.; Carter, M.; Matson, S.; Onley, C., 2001) My dad appears to have a lower risk profile based on reviewing validated risk assessment. Concerning actuarial risk factors; he did not have prior criminal history or sentencing dates, no prior sex offense charge or conviction, no prior violent conviction, no unrelated, stranger, or male victim. And, being married in a long term relationship was a protective factor.

Concerning dynamic risk factors, he had some protective factors in place. Significant positive social supports existed. He was in a committed intimate relationship. He was accepted and integrated into the community. He had permanent housing, steady employment, a lack of cognitive deficits, a lack of mental health illness, and his honorable discharge from the military would

---

[46] "People" Magazine Article; June 10th, 1991

indicate his ability to cooperate with authority and complete a program. (Hanson, R.K., Harris, A., 1998-01) If he failed to comply with requirements of a diversionary program, he could then be subject to criminal prosecution and penalties. This approach would have provided the early intervention needed, the accountability required, and a comprehensive, holistic approach to healing, keeping with what the literature identifies as a practical, healthy approach. Staying together as a family was a huge motivator for us. We wanted to stay together. We needed to stay together. However, we did not want to stay together as the dysfunctional, chaotic, abusive family. We wanted to become a healthy family. We wanted to be a caring, loving, and supportive family; like the families that mentored us from the Baptist church. We were able to accomplish this transformation through their involvement, and the involvement of people within the A.A. 12 Step community. We did not have legal, professional participation as children. However, much of the holistic healing began as we became involved in professional counseling services as adults.

I believe that a diversionary program like the one described would have brought the healing transformation around sooner for us. We all would have been getting the assistance and services we needed, individually and as a family. My dad's removal from the household (had this occurred), would have been as a temporary measure for protection in the earliest phase of treatment. Safe, healthy, constructive, and appropriate boundaries could have been developed and implemented, with the commitment of my parents to follow through, paired with professional clinical oversight.

A social worker would have had a case permanency plan with appropriate goals, timelines, and the review of juvenile court or family court services. I think that this type of approach would have been very appropriate, given what we know about intra-familial sexual abuse programs yielding successful outcomes. Does that undo the harm, or erase the trauma bonds and residual consequences that have plagued us throughout our adult lives? No; quite simply, it does not. Like many other survivors of incest and familial abuse, we have experienced our battles with substance abuse, dissociative disorders, post-traumatic stress disorders, weight disorders, and sexual dysfunction played out in various ways. Collectively, my siblings and I have amassed years of professional counseling and therapy to heal.

That reality was going to exist whether or not our father even faced prosecution. So, from our perspective, punishing him just for the sake of making him pay for his crimes would not have yielded a better outcome for us. Had he been sentenced to 10-25 years in prison with a "special sentence" parole, possibly for life, it was not going to alter our path that had to occur to heal. It would have removed him from the equation. The unintended collateral damage to our family, all for public safety and with good intentions, would have sent all of us on very different trajectories through life.

With what we know about incest abuse, incestuous sexual abusers, and the low rates of recidivism once identified, an approach like a diversionary program or deferred sentence with community supervision and required treatment would yield better results. Even a suspended sentence with community oversight and required treatment is a better approach than lengthy incarceration, enhanced penalties, and lifetime parole. I believe that in our case, the better results would have come whether the enforcing agency was the criminal court or the family court. The supervision could have come from either correctional services or social services. Both systems wield considerable power and authority within families. There are also many more non-professional support networks to partner with that are available within community-based correctional and social services agencies than prison programs have available for incarcerated offenders.

Two of those community resources from the non-professional network that proved invaluable for our family was a caring local church and the A.A. 12 Step community. Reaching out to the hurting, the broken, and those in need of assistance is synonymous to the core tenants of churches and recovery organizations. It is fulfilling the last step listed in the Big Book of Alcoholics Anonymous, "Having had a spiritual awakening as the result of these steps, we tried to carry this message to alcoholics, and to practice these principles in all our affairs." (Alcoholics Anonymous World Services, Inc., 1939, 1955, 1976, 2001). With proper training and waiver of confidentiality releases signed, these resources can successfully partner with professional services agencies to provide mentoring, sponsorship, circles of support and accountability (COSA)[47], and promote the healing process.

---

[47] Circles of Support & Accountability (COSA) is a term describing a team approach to mentoring, originating in Canadian treatment approaches in 1994 focused on restorative justice principles.

Do we need sex offender registries? Is public notification a necessity? Do we need formal prosecution? Do some criminals need to go to prison? Do some perpetrators need to be placed on probation? Do penalties need to be enhanced? Are sex offender treatment programs essential? Are sex offender management programs relevant? The answer to all of these questions is "yes", with caveats. Looking at sexual abuse and sexual abusers through the lenses of homogeneity, and trying to apply a "one size fits all" approach, yields poor results. Those poor results exist whether that is in the realm of legislation, prosecution, enforcement, or treatment. Understanding the complexities of sexual abuse, the heterogeneity of the sexual abusers, and developing individualized approaches based upon risk-need-response (RNR) principles will yield the better outcomes we are all striving for in sex offender management. Better results are especially true when we commit to implementing policies and strategies grounded in evidenced-based research.

In a speech in 1910, Winston Churchill stated, "The mood and temper of the public regarding the treatment of crime and criminals is one of the most unfailing tests of the civilization of any country."[48] Those words seem to be as important to consider for the politicians, legislators, criminal justice professionals, and the general public of today, as they were to Churchill and those in his day. Any decisions concerning what to do with sexual abusers and how the criminal justice system should deal with them must be well thought out. Decisions must involve research, planning, and execution with a deliberate conviction that demonstrates an awareness of the problem. An understanding of the specific needs for balancing public safety with rehabilitation is critical for success. It must involve decisions that promote healing for people, the individuals, the families, and entire communities.

I would be remiss to say that what would have probably worked with my family is the best or only approach with all families. That is not the case. Every family is different. And, their experiences with surviving trauma and abuse is different, too. Even within my family, there is not unanimous agreement on all of the views I have expressed here. I do not presume to speak for every family that has survived sexual abuse, or that I know what approach, or a combination of methods, would be most useful for their healing and restoration.

---

[48] This quote from Churchill was cited in a Congressional Senate Record concerning the Prison Rape Elimination Act of 2003

Around the same time frame that my sister disclosed her incest abuse to me, I was also piecing together a disturbing pattern that I thought existed with my wife (now former wife) and some of her family dynamics. One night as we were reading in bed, I told my wife that I was not sure of this, but that I had some concerns that she may have also survived some incest abuse as a child like my older sister had. I told her that she did not have to talk about it, however, if it was true, and she ever wanted to say, that I would listen. The floodgates opened, and what followed was her telling me of years of forced sexual abuse by a family member. She married her first husband at sixteen years old to flee and get away.

My wife wasn't ready to disclose her secret. The fact that I was bringing books, videos, and sexual abuse treatment materials home, and talking about it round the clock, seemed to force it upon her. As childhood memories and flashbacks flooded in, she struggled to deal with the emotions. I encourage her to seek professional counseling. I offered to go with her. She wasn't ready. Although many factors contributed to our eventual divorce, in my opinion, the trauma of her incest abuse played a significant role.

From the time the secret was out, a repeating theme in our marital conflict was how she felt that I did not love her. She felt that I would be better off without her. She felt that she was not good enough for me. Through a decade of marriage, I had known that she had also grown up in a dysfunctional family similar to mine. I did not know of her personal ordeal or her secret. Once disclosed, she now felt like "damaged goods." She struggled to believe that I could still somehow love her after knowing the truth. Divorce is complicated. Multiple factors are contributing to the ending of marriage. However, I cannot take the incest abuse off the table. It was a significant contributor to our marital collapse.

The diversionary program already mentioned would probably not have been very productive with my former wife's family. Multiple family members were alleging sexual abuse, as well as someone outside the household. There were step-family dynamics. There were dynamics within that family system that were different than what existed within my family. There were people within that family already involved with social services and correctional services. My wife's alleged perpetrator had a criminal history apart from the sexual abuse.

He (alleged perpetrator) recently passed away. My former wife initially wished he was in hell getting the kind of torture he had inflicted for years upon her and other young girls. He never took responsibility for the abuse. He denied it ever happened. The girls were all "liars, sluts, and whores", as he referred to them. I asked her if she would feel different had he even at least took responsibility for her abuse and apologized. Would it be different if he had asked for forgiveness and went on to have a safe, appropriate relationship with her? She shed tears and nodded in an affirming way. She did not want punishment and torture for this man. She wanted reconciliation. She wanted affirmation that she had not lied. She was not a whore. She was not a slut. It was not her fault. She wanted him to take responsibility for the harm he had inflicted upon her, and to show some desire toward making amends.

Incest abusers are not strangers. Abuse survivors have a relationship with these persons. Sometimes, these people are loving, caring, and protective. However, when given to the dark side of their nature, they are selfish, self-centered, and self-serving in their actions. When they finally admit that, and commit to repairing the harm the best that they can, many (although not all) of the survivors are receptive. They want healing and restoration of the family. Again, it is not universal. One size does not fit all.

It is important for providers to know and understand that this dynamic can be different for incest survivors than someone having an unrelated or stranger perpetrator. For intra-familial families of sexual abuse that do desire to stay together, and are even willing to go through the rigors of professional services to bring about healing, our legal system has made it tough. Hope of that quickly dissipates when the abuser faces sentencing to lengthy incarceration before ever being eligible for release to community supervision. For the families, the reality is that they must go on about living.

While I have my former wife's permission to share her being an incest abuse survivor and her comments I have shared, I have purposely omitted any names, family relationships, or identities of others. She no longer has my last name. I want to maintain anonymity and respect to all of the people involved. I'm merely trying to make a point.

Like the pebble in the pond that makes a splash and sends multiple ripples across the wake of the water, sexual abuse also impacts lives in complicated ways. The ripple effect affects entire family systems. Sometimes the residual consequences can last for generations. The decisions we make as the providers and managers having oversight of the abusers, as well as the families, will also have consequences which can last for generations.

We will not achieve successful outcomes through approaches that are at the extremes of the continuum and applied in a very homogenous way. We have learned through research and study that the majority of sexual abusers are not strangers, and most have little likelihood of sexual reoffending, once caught and given formal interventions. Many have some level of guilt, shame, and remorse over their actions. A confrontational dogmatic approach to treatment and supervision will impede progress. While it may bring partial compliance, it will not facilitate lasting change within a client's belief system.

As Geral Blanchard and other recognized sexual abuse treatment providers have noted, the healing manifests itself from the ability to establish a relationship with the abuser.[49] Building a positive relationship with the offender may be one of the biggest challenges facing sex offender treatment providers and supervision authorities, given the continuing trend to enact tougher laws, longer sentences, and harsher penalties for sexual abusers. In my experience as a sex offender treatment provider, this has been the trend since the establishment of national registries and public notification laws. Since the sweeping enactment of enhanced penalties across multiple jurisdictions that occurred this last decade, we've maybe taken the foot off the gas a little. We still appear to be heavy into punishment and enforcement, though. And, the highest risk profiles continue to set the stage for policies and decision-making about the group of sexual abusers as a whole.

If a program manager, therapist, or supervision officer, wants to err on the side of caution, for fear of answering for any decision made, punitive approaches will inevitably win out most of the time. The research has convincingly shown that for the lowest risk group of sexual abusers, these castigatory approaches may not only impede progress but actually, increase recidivism. (Lovins, Lowenkamp, & Latessa, 2009).[50]

---

[49] Note: Geral Blanchard, author of "The Difficult Connection: The Therapeutic Relationship in Sex Offender Treatment" (1995)

[50] These researchers found that high-risk offenders that completed intensive residential treatment were two times less likely to recidivate than high-risk offenders that did not complete intensive treatment. Low-risk offenders who received intensive treatment

I hope that this book has brought to light the complexities of these issues surrounding sexual abuse, sexual abusers, and familial abuse. And, that the individuals involved (abusers, direct victims, or indirect victims) are real, living, breathing people. We are all children of God created in His image. We are all in need of healing; in need of redemption. At the beginning of this book, I was able to tell you that I am not a sex offender. I am not able to inform you that I am not an abuser. I'm simply not a sexual abuser.

I have engaged in harmful behavior that hurt others. I injured people as a result of my violence. I caused pain to my family through my alcohol abuse. Some clinicians in my early treatment experiences diagnosed me as an alcoholic. Clinicians later have moved away from that label. They identified me as a young man acting out as a result of childhood trauma and reacting to my environment. When I truly healed, the desire to abuse alcohol or any substances, left me.

The label isn't necessary. The pain I caused other people is important. My responsibility to repair the harm is necessary. My commitment to living a better life is essential. Even sexual problems, and acting out that is not a crime, causes harm to other people. My committing adultery with married women damaged relationships. Families were hurt. I became a victim and subsequent survivor of my abuses. If this story resonates with you, or your family experiences, cling to faith and hope! If you work in this field, please remember what Jack told me; only do this job if you can see a human being across the desk from you, and you believe that people can change.

The Lakota have a saying, *"Mitakuye Oyasin"*; "we are all related; all of my relations; all of my relatives." It is used in prayers to describe our unity; connectedness; with each other and all life forms. We learn and grow together through pain and suffering; inflicted by us, and received upon us. We all are two sides of the same coin; abusers and abused; victim and victimizer (of something); that is our human condition. It is the Cherokee parable of two wolves. We all feed the evil wolf at times which brings harm to others as well as ourselves. This human condition does not give sexual abusers an excuse for the

---

recidivated at a rate of 21% higher than low-risk offenders' not placed in intensive treatment.

pain they have inflicted. It merely reminds us that they, too, are people responsible for repairing the harm that they have caused as best as they can.[51]

I have had a life enriched by the experiences of working with abusers and their families. I know that I have also had an impact on their lives in a positive way. It has been a part of my healing as well as theirs; paying it forward. My older sister, Rhonda, feels the same way. Before her physical disabilities forced her to retire, she loved her work in the nursing home. She gained fulfillment helping elderly patients and trying to make their remaining time in this life as happy and peaceful as possible. It brought healing to her, too.

One of those patients was her best friend's mother. The woman who let Rhonda stay overnight in high school and become a part of their family. Rhonda had the opportunity in many talks to thank her for her hospitality, kindness, and caring. She had the strength to tell this woman her long kept secret that only the inner circle and a college campus minister knew. Rhonda disclosed being an incest survivor and that the time spent in their home with a loving family meant more than anything words could describe. The woman cried, hugged her, and told her that she wished she would have known; she would have done something to help. She was a school teacher, and probably could have had such influence, maybe even back then. Rhonda explained all of the challenges and barriers to ever being able to tell her. The woman said she understood.

Rhonda had a similar experience in the last few years with an Aunt. They were talking one day and reminiscing. Rhonda found the strength also to disclose the incest to her. Our Aunt cried and also hugged her. She made a comment that she wished that she had only known. She told her that she loved us kids and surely would have done something to keep us safe. From what Rhonda has shared with me that disclosure has brought an even closer bond between them than was there before. If any of the Brewer Street kids has a right to be still angry; to be bitter; to be unforgiving; it is her. She is no longer stuck there either, though. She has moved from a victim of incest abuse to being a survivor of the familial abuse. She has forgiven Dad and Mom, and all of her siblings for not ever understanding. She believes in Romans 8:28 and quotes it

---

[51] AA 12 Step principles; specifically steps 8-9-10

often.[52] She knows that God will use all things for good for those that love Him and desire to serve Him. Even the horrible experiences of familial abuse and incest.

Rhonda is excited about this book and hopeful it will be published. She spent hours collaborating with me and sharing her thoughts, feelings, and insights. This book has been a journey of healing for both of us. My former wife is also excited about the book. She and I have had numerous talks over food and fellowship to discuss her ordeal. She has opened up more in these last few months than she had in the prior twenty years since the initial disclosure that night reading in bed.

If no one reads the book, it has been worth it just for the healing it has brought to us; the "Brewer Street Kids" and my former wife. The value of that is priceless! It has allowed the direct survivors of the incest abuse to share their story with others in a way they did not feel comfortable doing on their own. When I set out to write this book, I mistakenly thought that I had completely healed from my pain of surviving familial abuse. This massive undertaking reminded me, the professional treatment provider, that healing and recovery are lifelong journeys which never stop. We are never completely healed; it is a progression from brokenness to wellness. We believe that there is healing in the stories and messages written within these pages. We pray that God will use this work for the healing of others.

I have prayed about this book not being a reflection of just a "Poor me, feel sorry for the boy that endured some appalling things. Isn't that a shame." This thought does run through my head. I frequently confront the thought, "Grow up, Randy. You're nearly 60 years old. Move on and get over it." I remind myself that I did grow up and move on. In some ways, I did get over it. In other ways, I can't get over it. It is woven into the fabric of who I am. The difference for me is, instead of allowing it to destroy me like I was doing as a young man, I have allowed it to inspire me. I have found redemption. Thank you, Lord. Amen.

I was recently having lunch with a friend who is a mentor and professional colleague. We talked about many things, one of which was the status of this book. We shared stories of our youth; the relationships with our dads'. At one

---

[52] Romans 8:28; "We know that God is always at work for the good of everyone that loves Him." (CEV)

point he paused and reflected. He commented it was interesting at nearly sixty years old; the emotional pain still surfaces in conversations. For me, the pain of growing up without the approval of my father continues to surface. I needed his support, albeit the backing of a sexual abuser.

Reducing my dad to a label of "sex offender", or "child molester" is not an accurate portrayal of him, nor does it recognize the complexities to the recovery process for my siblings and me. Our struggle to heal is diminished in a simple label. He was an auspicious Marine. He was a skilled mechanic and machinist. He was an excellent fisherman, hunter, and outdoorsman. He brought coon hound pups into the house and placed them in little beds made with towels and pop flats, placing them on top of the stove for the heat to save them. He bottle-fed baby squirrels and raccoons abandoned or orphaned, to release them back into the wild when they were old enough to survive. I fell through the ice as a boy in the winter. I was up to my waist in water and had to walk home; nearly three miles in freezing temperatures. He knew to warm my legs up gradually and stayed up all night to massage them. The doctor credited early intervention to the frostbite being mild.

My father was a human being. A man that sadly had a problem with sexual, and physical acting out behaviors that were harmful. The deepest wounds, though are emotional scars. They do last a lifetime. Not as intense now; not as frequent; no longer debilitating. It is much more of a humble acknowledgment; it was what it was, and nothing will change that. That thought follows by a liberating gratitude that it did not stay that way. We all chose to heal and not allow any labels to define us, my father included. We all must learn to feed the real irrefutable right wolf and let the fruits of the Spirit dwell within us; God's nature that exists in us to counter the flesh. These fruits living within us will then flow from us; "God's Spirit makes us loving, happy, peaceful, patient, kind, good, faithful, gentle, and self-controlled."[53] Understanding that process will promote healing. Labeling and dividing us will not. God desires unity within all of His creation. God bless your journey. Thank you for reading *The Boy Under the Bed*.

---

[53] Galatians, Chapter 5:22-23 (CEV)

"It is when we attempt to impose the dominant paradigm, where one size fits all, that we often fashion a poor fit that slows and even prevents growth."

Geral Blanchard,
Ancient Ethics for Today's Healers

Figure 17: The Brewer Street Kids, April 2016.

Figure 18: Family photo about one year before Dad died; circa, 1999

Figure 19: Me at my heaviest; about 300 lbs.; Sibling photo, 2012

Figure 20: Food was a comfort. I weighed about 300 lbs. when I elected to have a gastric sleeve in 2013. I now weigh about 178 pounds.

Figure 21: Me with the oldest son; 1999

Figure 22: Me with the youngest son; 1999

Figure 23: My sons; youngest son's wedding, 2007

Figure 24: you would think a big guy would have a big dog?
Grandma Nellie had JRT's. My terrier,
Tillie, reminds me of her; circa, 2010

Figure 25: Vacation with oldest son & granddaughter; Grant's Farm, St. Louis (2016). My cousins drove the hitch for many years.

Figure 26: John Wayne; one of my childhood heroes. (2015)

Figure 27: About as lean as when I separated from active duty; 179 lbs.

Figure 28: Recent photo; as healthy as I have ever been! (2016)

Figure 29: St. Joseph's Indian School Pow-Wow, 2013. Older Sister & I both support the Lakota children.

Figure 30: The premature babies, all grown up! (2015)

Figure 31: Dad was an amazing outdoorsman! He especially loved hunting ginseng; circa, 1978

Figure 32: Mom and me, shortly before she passed away; 2011

REFERENCES

Adam Walsh Child Protection and Safety Act. (n.d.) Retrieved June 14, 2016, from https://en.wikipedia.org/wiki/Adam_Walsh_Child_Protection_and_Safety_Act

Alcoholics Anonymous World Services, Inc. (1939, 1955, 1976, 2001). *Alcoholics Anonymous, Fourth Edition.* New York: Alcoholics Anonymous World Services, Inc.

Army Aircraft Post-War Deaths in Korea. (2002-2016). Korean War Educator. Retrieved from: http://koreanwar-educator.org/topics/dmz/p_dmz_Army_aircraft_postwar_deaths.htm

Bailey, V. (1985) Churchill as Home Secretary. *History Today.* Vol.35. Issue 3

Blanchard, G. (2014). *Ancient Ethics for Today's Healers.* Holyoke: NEARI Press.

Blanchard, G. (1995). *The Difficult Connection: The Therapeutic Relationship in Sex Offender Treatment.* Brandon. Brandon: Safer Society Press.

Bradshaw, J. (1988, 2005). *Healing the Shame that Binds You.* Deerfield Beach: Health Communications, Inc.

Bynum, T.; Carter,M.; Matson, S.; Onley,C. (2001). *Recidivism of Sex Offenders.* Silver Spring: Center for Sex Offender Management .

Circles of Support and Accountability. (2016) Retrieved from: https://en.wikipedia.org/wiki/Circles_of_Support_and_Accountability

CSOM National Resource Group. (2008). *The Comprehensive Approach to Sex Offender Management .* Silver Spring: Center for Sex Offender Management .

Dealer's Choice. (1972). Parker Brothers Board Game. Retrieved from: https://boardgamegeek.com/boardgame/1434/dealers-choice

Freeman-Longo, R., Blanchard, G. (1998). *Sexual Abuse in America: Epidemic of the 21st Century.* Brandon: Safer Society Press

Fischer, H. (2007). *North Korean Provocative Actions, 1950-2007.* CRS Report for Congress. Retrieved from: https://fas.org/sgp/crs/row/RL30004.pdf

Glass. (2010). Reagan declares "War on Drugs", October 14, 1982. *Politico.*

Hall, Pete; Simeral, Alisa. (2015). *Teach, Reflect, Learn : Building Your Capacity for Success in the Classroom.* Alexandria: ASCD. Retrieved from http://www.eblib.com.

Hanson, R.K., Harris, A. (1998-01). *Dynamic Predictors of Sexual Recidivism- Corrections Research User Report.* Ottawa: Solicitor General Canada.

Hanson, R.K.; Harris, A.; Phenix, A.; Thorton,D. . (2003). *Static 99 Coding Rules-Revised 2003.* Ottawa: Solicitor General Canada.

Herman, J. (1981). *Father-Daughter Incest.* Cambridge: Harvard University Press.

Holy Bible. (1995). *Contemporary English Version.* New York. American Bible Society.

Hynes, P. H. (2013). The Korean War: Forgotten, Unknown, and Unfinished. *Truthout.*

Junger, S. (2016). *Tribe: On Homecoming and Belonging.* New York: Hachette Book Group, Inc.

Knowles, M., Holton, E. F., & A., S. R. (2012). *The Adult Learner.* New York: Taylor and Francis.

List of Border Incidents Involving North Korea. (n.d.) Retrieved June 19, 2016, from https://en.wikipedia.org/wiki/List_of_border_incidents_involving_North_Korea

Lovins, Lowenkamp, & Latessa. (2009). Applying the risk principle to sex offenders: Can treatment make some sex offenders worse? *The Prison Journal,* pp. 344-357.

McDorman, M. R. (1993). Trends in infant mortali~by cause of death. *National Center for Health Statistics. Vital,* 57.

Monopoly. (1935). Parker Brothers Board Game. Retrieved from: https://en.wikipedia.org/wiki/Monopoly (game)

Prell. (2010). *Statistical Validation of the ISORA-8 and STATIC 99*. Des Moines: Iowa Department of Corrections.

Rummy Royal. (1965). Whitman Board Game. Retrieved from:
http://www.rarityguide.com/museum/card_and_board_games/rummy_royal__whitman_1965_/rummy_royal_whitman_1965_playing_mat/

Russell, S. S. (2006). An Overview of Adult Learning Processes. *Medscape Multispeciality*, 349-352, 370.

Sole Survivor Policy. (2016). Retrieved July 10, 2016, from
https://en.wikipedia.org/wiki/Sole_Survivor_Policy

Sorry. (1934). Parker Brothers Board Game. Retrieved from:
https://en.wikipedia.org/wiki/Sorry!_(game)

The Learning Network. (2012, April 30). April 30, 1975: Saigon Falls. *New York Times.*

The Oprah Winfrey Show.(2005, June 13). Harpo Studios Productions. Chicago, Illinois, United States of America.

Van Debur Atlar, M. (1991). The Darkest Secret. *People Magazine*, Vol.35, No.22.

WORKS CITED

Alcoholics Anonymous World Services, Inc. (1939, 1955, 1976, 2001). *Alcoholics Anonymous, Fourth Edition.* New York: Alcoholics Anonymous World Services, Inc.

Blanchard, G. (2014). *Ancient Ethics for Today's Healers.* Holyoke: NEARI Press.

Bradshaw, J. (1988, 2005). *Healing the Shame that Binds You.* Deerfield Beach: Health Communications, Inc.

Bynum, T.; Carter,M.; Matson, S.; Onley,C. (2001). *Rcidivism of Sex Offenders.* Silver Spring: Center for Sex Offender Management .

Circles of Support and Accountability. (2016) Retrieved from: https://en.wikipedia.org/wiki/Circles_of_Support_and_Accountability

CSOM National Resource Group. (2008). *The Comprehensive Approach to Sex Offender Management.* Silver Spring: Center for Sex Offender Management .

Glass. (2010). Reagan declares "War on Drugs", October 14, 1982. *Politico.*

Hall, Pete; Simeral, Alisa. (2015). *Teach, Reflect, Learn : Building Your Capacity for Success in the Classroom.* Alexandria: ASCD. Retrieved from http://www.eblib.com.

Hanson, R.K., Harris, A. (1998-01). *Dynamic Predictors of Sexual Recidivism- Corrections Research User Report.* Ottawa: Solicitor General Canada.

Hanson, R.K.; Harris, A.; Phenix, A.; Thorton,D. . (2003). *Static 99 Coding Rules-Revised 2003.* Ottawa: Solicitor General Canada.

Herman, J. (1981). *Father-Daughter Incest.* Cambridge: Harvard University Press.

Holy Bible. (1995). *Contemporary English Version.* New York. American Bible Society.

Hynes, P. H. (2013). The Korean War: Forgotten, Unknown, and Unfinished. *Truthout.*

Junger, S. (2016). *Tribe: On Homecoming and Belonging*. New York: Hachette Book Group, Inc.

Knowles, M., Holton, E. F., & A., S. R. (2012). *The Adult Learner*. New York: Taylor and Francis.

Lovins, Lowenkamp, & Latessa. (2009). Applying the risk principle to sex offenders: Can treatment make some sex offenders worse? *The Prison Journal*, pp. 344-357.

McDorman, M. R. (1993). Trends in infant mortali~ by cause of death. *National Center for Health Statistics. Vital*, 57.

Prell. (2010). *Statistical Validation of the ISORA-8 and STATIC 99*. Des Moines: Iowa Department of Corrections.

Russell, S. S. (2006). An Overview of Adult Learning Processes. *Medscape Multispeciality*, 349-352, 370.

The Learning Network. (2012, April 30). April 30, 1975: Saigon Falls. *New York Times*.

The Oprah Winfrey Show. (2005, June 13). Harpo Studios Productions. Chicago, Illinois, United States of America.

Van Debur Atlar, M. (1991). The Darkest Secret. *People Magazine*, Vol.35, No.22.

BIBLIOGRAPHY

Adam Walsh Child Protection and Safety Act. (n.d.) Retrieved June 14, 2016, from
https://en.wikipedia.org/wiki/Adam_Walsh_Child_Protection_and_Saf
ety_Act

Alcoholics Anonymous World Services, Inc. (1939, 1955, 1976, 2001). *Alcoholics
Anonymous, Fourth Edition.* New York: Alcoholics Anonymous World
Services, Inc.

Army Aircraft Post-War Deaths in Korea. (2002-2016). Korean War Educator.
Retrieved from: http://koreanwar-
educator.org/topics/dmz/p_dmz_Army_aircraft_postwar_deaths.htm

Bailey, V. (1985) Churchill as Home Secretary. *History Today.* Vol.35. Issue 3

Blanchard, G. (2014). *Ancient Ethics for Today's Healers.* Holyoke: NEARI Press.

Blanchard, G. (1995). *The Difficult Connection: The Therapeutic Relationship in Sex
Offender Treatment.* Brandon: Safer Society Press.

Bradshaw, J. (1988, 2005). *Healing the Shame that Binds You.* Deerfield Beach: Health
Communications, Inc.

Bynum, T.; Carter, M.; Matson, S.; Onley, C. (2001). *Recidivism of Sex Offenders.* Silver
Spring: Center for Sex Offender Management.

Cambell, Glen. (1968) *Wichita Lineman Album.* Retrieved June 14, 2016, from
https://www.discogs.com/Glen-Campbell-Wichita-
Lineman/master/152001

Chadbourne, Eugene. (n.d.) *All Music Review-Loretta Lynn.* Retrieved June 14, 2016,
from http://www.allmusic.com/album/dont-come-home-a-drinkin-with-
lovin-on-your-mind-mw0000691675

Child Abuse Prevention and Treatment Act. (n.d.) Retrieved June 14, 2016, from
https://en.wikipedia.org/wiki/Child_Abuse_Prevention_and_Treatment
_Act

Child Sexual Abuse. (n.d.) Retrieved June 14, 2016, from
https://en.wikipedia.org/wiki/Child_sexual_abuse

Circles of Support and Accountability. (2016) Retrieved from:
https://en.wikipedia.org/wiki/Circles_of_Support_and_Accountability

Cook, Stephen. (n.d.) *All Music Review-Tammy Wynette.* Retrieved June 14, 2016, from
http://www.allmusic.com/album/20-greatest-hits-mw0000083976

CSOM National Resource Group. (2008). *The Comprehensive Approach to Sex
Offender Management.* Silver Spring: Center for Sex Offender Management.

Dealer's Choice. (1972). Parker Brothers Board Game. Retrieved from:
https://boardgamegeek.com/boardgame/1434/dealers-choice

Fischer, H. (2007). *North Korean Provocative Actions, 1950-2007.* CRS Report for
Congress. Retrieved from: https://fas.org/sgp/crs/row/RL30004.pdf

Freeman-Longo, R., Blanchard, G. (1998). *Sexual Abuse in America: Epidemic of the
21st Century.* Brandon: Safer Society Press

Glass. (2010). Reagan declares "War on Drugs," October 14, 1982. *Politico.*

Hall, Pete; Simeral, Alisa. (2015). *Teach, Reflect, Learn: Building Your Capacity for
Success in the Classroom.* Alexandria: ASCD. Retrieved from
http://www.eblib.com.

Hanson, R.k., Harris, A. (1998-01). *Dynamic Predictors of Sexual Recidivism- Corrections
Research User Report.* Ottawa: Solicitor General Canada.

Hanson, R.K.; Harris, A.; Phenix, A.; Thorton, D. (2003). *Static 99 Coding Rules-
Revised 2003.* Ottawa: Solicitor General Canada.

Herman, J. (1981). *Father-Daughter Incest.* Cambridge: Harvard University Press.

Holy Bible. (1995). *Contemporary English Version.* New York. American Bible Society.

Hynes, P. H. (2013). The Korean War: Forgotten, Unknown, and Unfinished.
Truthout.

Junger, S. (2016). *Tribe: On Homecoming and Belonging*. New York: Hachette Book Group, Inc.

Knowles, M., Holton, E. F., & A., S. R. (2012). *The Adult Learner*. New York: Taylor and Francis.

List of Border Incidents Involving North Korea. (n.d.) Retrieved June 19, 2016, from https://en.wikipedia.org/wiki/List_of_border_incidents_involving_Nort h_Korea

Lovins, Lowenkamp, & Latessa. (2009). Applying the risk principle to sex offenders: Can treatment make some sex offenders worse? *The Prison Journal*, pp. 344-357.

McDorman, M. R. (1993). Trends in infant mortali~ by cause of death. *National Center for Health Statistics. Vital*, 57.

Mitakuye Oyasin. (n.d.) Retrieved June 14, 2016, from https://en.wikipedia.org/wiki/Mitakuye_Oyasin

McMartin Preschool Trial. (n.d.). Retrieved June 14, 2016, from https://en.wikipedia.org/wiki/McMartin_preschool_trial

Monopoly. (1935). Parker Brothers Board Game. Retrieved from: https://en.wikipedia.org/wiki/Monopoly_(game)

Prell. (2010). *The Statistical Validation of the ISORA-8 and STATIC 99*. Des Moines: Iowa Department of Corrections.

Prison Rape Elimination Act. (n.d.) Retrieved June 14, 2016, from https://en.wikipedia.org/wiki/Prison_Rape_Elimination_Act_of_2003

Rummy Royal. (1965). Whitman Board Game. Retrieved from: http://www.rarityguide.com/museum/card_and_board_games/rummy_ royal__whitman_1965_/rummy_royal_whitman_1965_playing_mat/

Russell, S. S. (2006). An Overview of Adult Learning Processes. *Medscape Multispeciality*, 349-352, 370.

Sole Survivor Policy. (2016). Retrieved July 10, 2016, from https://en.wikipedia.org/wiki/Sole_Survivor_Policy

Sorry. (1934). Parker Brothers Board Game. Retrieved from:
https://en.wikipedia.org/wiki/Sorry!_(game)

The Learning Network. (2012, April 30). April 30, 1975: Saigon Falls. *New York Times.*

The Oprah Winfrey Show. (2005, June 13). Harpo Studios Productions. Chicago, Illinois, United States of America.

Van Debur Atlar, M. (1991). The Darkest Secret. *People Magazine,* Vol.35, No.22.

ABOUT THE AUTHOR

Figure 33: Photo used with permission, copyright Lifetouch,

Randy E. Cole, retired from the 6th Judicial District Department of Correctional Services-Iowa, in December 2014. He has worked in Human Services & Correctional Services for over 35 years. Mr. Cole is a certified Sex Offender Treatment Provider, Level II, and Past Chairperson of the Iowa Board for the Treatment of Sexual Abusers (IBTSA). He currently is the sole proprietor of R. Cole Consulting, LLC; a private investigation/polygraph service and consulting business. He is a Master Trainer certified by Dr. Karl Hanson, Solicitor General, Public Safety, Canada through the Dynamic Supervision Project (DSP) of Sex Offenders; a collaborative multi-jurisdictional study to validate the STATIC 99, 99-R, STABLE 2007, and ACUTE 2007 sex offender risk assessment instruments. It is one of the most comprehensive and widely used sex offender specific risk assessment formats currently available in the field. Mr. Cole has also been a national trainer and consultant in sex offender risk assessment and sex offender management since 2004. He has collaborated with other sex offender specialists through projects sponsored by the Center for Sex Offender Management (CSOM), Council of State Governments (CSG), as well as other national, state, and local agencies. Mr. Cole has an Associate's Degree in Human Services from Kirkwood Community College. He has a Bachelor's Degree from Mount Mercy University in Criminal Justice Administration. The author is currently pursuing Graduate Studies. Mr. Cole is a member of the following professional organizations:

- Association for the Treatment of Sexual Abusers (ATSA)
- Mn-ATSA (Minnesota chapter of ATSA)
- Iowa Board for the Treatment of Sexual Abusers (IBTSA)
- American Polygraph Association (APA)
- American Association for Adult Continuing Education (AAACE)

- Cedar Valley Detachment, Marine Corps League
- American Association of Retired Persons (AARP)

He is a certified lay speaker providing pulpit fill since the early 1990's. He has served on some amazing mission trips and as a volunteer chaplain in a hospital setting since 2009. Hobbie's & Leisure interests include golfing, tennis, bicycling, motorcycling, reading, fishing, hunting, and spending time with his family, grandchildren, and friends. He enjoys sweat lodge ceremonies and Native American spiritual healing traditions.
Website: https://www.RColeConsultingLLC.com

CPSIA information can be obtained
at www.ICGtesting.com
Printed in the USA
LVHW04s2137111018
593270LV00002BA/456/P